"Poetry matters and this book shows us why. The astonishing range of *Rue Rilke*—a travel diary, a meditation on Rilke, and a gripping account of efforts to oppose an unjust judicial execution—reveals the essense of what James Hillman calls soul-making. Poet, essayist, and passionate abolitionist, Daniel Polikoff gives us a book dedicated to the fiery poetry of life itself."

SUSAN ROWLAND
Author of *Jung as a Writer* and
The Ecocritical Psyche

"Diary, travelogue, poetic exercise; philosophical meditation, political manifesto, existential essay: *Rue Rilke* charts a new course in the world of letters. Well-known European and American places become sites of meditation rehearsing humankind's attempt to affirm life in the face of adversity and chaos. Combining prophecy and activism, *Rue Rilke* prods the imaginative heart to take a stand against the erasure of beauty and goodness, against the slumber of indifference and oblivion. In musing begins responsibility."

MARIE LIÉNARD-YETERIAN
University of Nice, France

ALSO BY DANIEL JOSEPH POLIKOFF

POETRY

The Hands of Stars

Dragon Ship

TRANSLATION

Parzival/Gawain: Two Plays
an edited translation of *Der Gral* by A.M. Miller

Sonnets to Orpheus
Rilke

CRITICISM

In the Image of Orpheus: Rilke—A Soul History

RUE RILKE

Daniel Joseph Polikoff

CHIRON PUBLICATIONS • ASHEVILLE, NORTH CAROLINA

www.ChironPublicatons.com

978-1-63051-358-0 paperback

978-1-63051-359-7 hardcover

978-1-63051-360-3 eBook

Cover design and typesetting by Nelly Murariu

Printed in the United States of America.

Library of Congress Cataloging-in-Publication Data

Names: Polikoff, Daniel Joseph, 1957- author.

Title: Rue Rilke / Daniel Joseph Polikoff.

Description: Asheville, N.C. : Chiron Publications, 2016. | Includes
  bibliographical references and index.

Identifiers: LCCN 2016010922 (print) | LCCN 2016022775 (ebook) | ISBN
  9781630513597 (hbk : alk. paper) | ISBN 9781630513580 (pbk : alk. paper) |
  ISBN 9781630513603 (eBook) | ISBN 9781630513603 (E-book)

Subjects: LCSH: Capital punishment--Texas. | Discrimination in criminal
  justice administration--Texas. | Discrimination in criminal justice
  administration--Illinois. | France--Description and travel. |
  Switzerland--Description and travel. | Rilke, Rainer Maria, 1875-1926.

Classification: LCC HV8699.U6 T46 2016 (print) | LCC HV8699.U6 (ebook) |
DDC

  364.6609764--dc23

LC record available at https://lccn.loc.gov/2016010922

Acknowledgments

It is rather unusual to publish a book 20 years after it was written, and this circumstance rather thins the ranks of those whom I might wish to acknowledge here. I do, however, wish to thank Len Cruz and Steve Buser at Chiron Publications for their continuing interest in my work and their support of the unique venture that is *Rue Rilke*. Jennifer Fitzgerald at Chiron helped guide the publication of the work with skill and patience. The Lubbock Avalanche-Journal, the Rothko Chapel, and Scott Langley all contributed valuable photographs, and I extend special thanks to the latter for his superb Death Penalty Photography Documentary Project. I owe a debt of gratitude as well to Susan Rowland, Bruce Bond, Naomi Lowinski, and Marie Liénard-Yeterian for taking the time necessary to read and respond to the book. Lastly, my thanks are due to the translators and publishers listed below.

Permissions

"On Every Christmas her first love returns to her mind" by Gaspara Stampa, translated by Frank Warnke, from *Three Women Poets of the Renaissance and Baroque*. Copyright (c) 1987 by Frank Warnke; reprinted by permission of Associated University Presses.

Excerpt from pp. 103-104 of *The Gospel According to Jesus* by Stephen Mitchell. Copyright (c) 1991 by Stephen Mitchell. Reprinted by permission of HarperCollins Publishers.

"Requiem for a Friend," translation copyright (c) 1982 by Stephen Mitchell: from *Selected Poetry of Rainer Maria Rilke* by Rainer Maria Rilke, translated by Stephen Mitchell. Used by permission of Random House, an imprint and division of Penguin Random House. LLC. All rights reserved.

"To Withold Huleciwz, November 10, 1925" from *The Notebooks of Malte Laurids Brigge: A Novel* by Rainer Maria Rilke, translated by Stephen Mitchell, translation copyright (c) 1982, 1983 by Stephen Mitchell. Used by permission of Random House, an imprint and division of Penguin Random House LLC. All rights reserved.

Contents

Preface

It has been two decades since I completed *Rue Rilke*, the literary diary-turned-book that chronicles my travels to France, Switzerland, Houston and Chicago in the summer of 1993. The European part of the journey unfolds my quest for more intimate knowledge of Rainer Maria Rilke himself, the poet whom I adopt as a spiritual guide; knowledge that is immediately and severely tested in the crucible of anti-death penalty activities deep in the heart of Texas. The introduction (written shortly after the narrated events) places the journey within an autobiographical context. Here, I would like to add a few words of explanation as to why I feel moved to make this work available to a wider audience now, after a hiatus of 20 years.

Rue Rilke gives voice and form to the inspiration I drew from my own discovery of Rilke at a relatively young age (younger in soul, perhaps, than in years). Since that time, my engagement with the writer has deepened and born riper fruit; even so, *Rue Rilke* represents the seedtime of my transformative relation to modernity's Orphic poet. Coincidently, while *Rue Rilke* does not mention the brilliantly iconoclastic psychologist by name, the same holds true with respect to James Hillman and his influential archetypal psychology. Reading *Rue Rilke* again after so many years, I am startled to discover how clearly the outlines of my still developing worldview are sketched—swiftly and decisively, if unevenly—here. Sober age and the slow forge of thought may make for substantial work, but the impetuous fire of youth offers its own brand of insight. If my later *In the Image of Orpheus: Rilke—A Soul History* represents a solid accomplishment, that senex tome may be well complemented by an earlier, more combustible exploration that lives and breathes the air of the archetypal *puer aeternus*.

So much for the autobiographical and archetypal psycho-logical angles: Political history also contributes to my interest in publishing the book at this juncture. Recent developments—most signally, the killing of Michael Brown in Ferguson, Missouri, and a spate of other news-grabbing instances of white-on-black violence—has once more thrust the issue of racial discrimination into the spotlight of American public conscience. *Rue Rilke* has a great deal to do with this charged and strife-ridden terrain, for the book is not only a search for the roots of Rilke's imaginative consciousness amid his own European haunts. The second, American part of the story aims—with the improbable audacity proper to youth—to bring the insight thus gained home to bear on one of the most intractable problems of American politics: namely, the death penalty. This part finds me traveling to Houston to bear witness to the unfolding legal and human drama of Gary Graham, a young Black man scheduled for imminent execution—a legal and human drama in which images of *Black* and *White* play a leading role. While formal executions and police violence are not exactly identical phenomena, I do not think it is too hard to see that these kindred instances of state-sanctioned lethal force may well arise from the same deeply unconscious source.

Let me close this preface with a brief word on some of the poems and translations that appear in the text. While I have recently published a translation of Rilke's *Sonnets to Orpheus*, some early versions of these efforts appear in *Rue Rilke*, and I have left these in their raw original form. The reader will find a larger number of kindred sonnets that (to those familiar with the Rilkean originals) will rightly appear not so much *translated* as rather radically and strangely *transformed* or metamorphosed. Inspired by both Rilke's sonnets and Hillmans' *Myth of Analysis*, I composed a sonnet sequence (*Sonnets to Psyche;* abbreviated *SP*) that effectively transfigures Rilke's own so that the poems reflect—not so much the myth of Orpheus and Eurydice—but rather that of Psyche and Eros. These poems—like the whole rich tapestry that is *Rue Rilke*—date from another epoch of my life and may occasionally sound as if they come from another era altogether. Yet in this age of smartphones and hashtags, perhaps the need to be reminded of the possibility of more poetic pasts—and futures!—is all the more pressing. As Rilke writes:

> *Are we really so fearful, so brittle-willed*
> *as fate would have us believe?*
> *Is childhood—so deep, so promise-filled—*
> *later stilled, root and leaf?*
>
> *Oh, the spectre of transience—*
> *through the heart's open innocence*
> *it moves, like smoke over light.*
>
> *As that which we are—driven and driving—*
> *we still count among the surviving*
> *powers as divine rite.*

—*Daniel Joseph Polikoff*
Mill Valley, California
April 14, 2015

O rose

shorn too soon

your petals now are strewn

everywhere

your beauty endless

In cherished Memory
of my Beloved sister
Joan Myra Polikoff

Introduction

I began reading Rilke about three years ago, after a devastating period I call my own dark ages. The travail of the doctoral dissertation coincided with a fracturing divorce, and the combination proved too much for me; I went under. Where, exactly, I went, and how long I stayed there is difficult to say; what is most important now is that, like a loon on a long dark lake, I came up far off from where I had been. And Rilke—well, perhaps no human being can tell where a diving bird might rise— but at least the poet had taken his own plunge into the element of soul and emerged with a voice instinct with its uncanny depths.

Our marriage was over almost before it was begun; three years after the fact my wife and I finally obtained a formal divorce. It was shortly afterward that I truly began my life again, for it was then that I began to write—not as a scholar—but as a poet. And this required a mentor, a guide; it required Rilke. And Rilke, in turn, required me to change my life.

> And let me here promptly make a request: Read as little as possible of aesthetic criticism—such things are either partisan views, petrified and grown senseless in their lifeless induration, or they are clever quibblings in which today one view wins and tomorrow the opposite. Works of art are of an infinite loneliness and with nothing so little to be reached as with criticism. Only love can grasp and hold and be just towards them.

Discontent with the unpoetical canons of criticism had long simmered beneath my work in Cornell's Department of Comparative Literature; Rilke's words set it aflame. Even as I was finally completing my doctoral dissertation, Rilke's letters and poems were turning me toward more imaginative literary vocation. I considered the conversion poetic justice, fair recompense for the manner in which my relation to literature had been stamped by an academic ideology inimical to the affections of the soul.

Jacques Derrida's visit to Cornell a short while before my dissertation defense signaled the sea change. Derrida was lecturing on the metaphysics of death; the huge auditorium at Cornell was overflowing, and the great thinker introduced (with no loss of ceremony) by Cornell's own critical dignitaries. Despite the aura of importance, it took no more than a few moments before I knew that Derrida had nothing to say to me: his words, while cleverly conceived, seemed to me utterly devoid of psychological life and rang as hollow as a drained glass. I was sitting far back in the auditorium, next to a mother holding an infant. I turned away from the lectern, watched the child for some time, rose, and left the hall.

> Be in advance of all parting, as if it were behind
> you, like the winter just gone by.
> For among winters there is one so endlessly winter
> that, in enduring it, your heart leaves time behind.
>
> Be forever dead in Eurydice—climb more singingly,
> more praisingly back in the pure relation.
> Here, in the midst of vanishing things, be, in the realm of decline,
> be a ringing glass that shatters even as it rings.

We appreciate most that which is gone from us, and a longing for that which is not presently possessed is essential to the experience of Love, as well as the poems that are among Eros' fairest offspring. It was no mere accident that Orpheus (that archetypal figure of poetry) lost his Eurydice to Hades not once, but twice, for it is difficult to imagine the lyre resounding through the ages in quite the same way if that mythic figure had not turned and (his grasping eyes unattuned to the flickering shadows) sent his beloved back to densest darkness where, like a nightingale, she could call forth mourning song from him forever. At least, I do not think I would have been so touched by the echoing chords if the script had been differently composed; if I had not been rent after marriage and been forced to seek in the dark, otherworldly mirror of verse the image of what had been lost (or, perhaps, never quite found) in life.

And it was there—there on the threshold, that I met Rilke, herald of the healing cosmogony of the poetic word, sounder of the call to poetic vocation. Orphic poet par excellence, Rilke took his art to heart like a beloved mistress; or rather, knew his words the sealed letters sent her in the night, the missives bearing now one name, and now another (Merline, Benvenuta, Marina, Lou-Lou, Lou) but always dedicated to that one Eurydice that held the answer to Love's illimitable call, that *psyche,* that *anima,* that was his very soul.

And so, following Rilke's Orphic footsteps, I began to write: translating his cycle of sonnets, retracing the lines that composed the journey of his life. And the soul-voyage thus begun was to take me many places, some of which seemed distant mirrors, while others appeared close-ups of home, though as time went on, far and near became more and more confused.

When I scheduled my departure for France and for Switzerland, I knew I would be leaving the university behind; though abroad for less than a month, I did not know when (if ever) I would return. Having defended the doctoral dissertation that had long been the albatross around my neck, I was free to consider my recent afternoon in Cornell's Fine Arts Library a kind of send-off, the augury— half-curse, half-blessing—traditionally bestowed upon a young man setting forth to seek his fortune in the world.

I had seen the article about Gary Graham's case several days before in *The New York Times;* interested in capital punishment, it struck me forcibly at the time. I put it in my current business folder to look at later, not really expecting to have much time for it on account of my upcoming journey. I was looking forward (among other things) to seeing the famous medieval tapestry *The Lady and the Unicorn*— which had meant so much to Rilke—in Paris. Anxious for a preview, I went to Cornell's Fine Arts Library to find a color reproduction. Sunk in contemplation of the pictures, I opened my folder to jot a note or two and suddenly Graham's face was there, alongside the tapestry. It would be difficult to conjure two more disparate images, two more distant worlds—on the one hand, the delicate, colorful medieval weave of *La Dame á la Licorne;* on the other, the black and white photo of a young African American scheduled for imminent execution in Texas. Yet the images did not—as one might have expected—clash and repel; rather, like two poles of one magnet, they seemed to exercise an irresistible attraction upon each other, so that the space of their small yet irreconcilable remove generated a field of immense force, an invisible vortex of unknown dimensions.

Without knowing what was happening, I was drawn in— dragged into the midst of the charged space as if I were a scattering of iron filings pulled between those poles— pulled, dragged, torn, and (sometimes, perhaps) held in fine suspension, a slim bridge spanning the space of invisible power.

Do not, then, be taken in by literary convention; the words you are reading are not a book I have written; these words *are* those filings; this text, a tapestry of thin iron bars concealing, and revealing, a face.

～

Shortly before 9:30 p.m. on May 13, 1981, Bobby Lambert, a middle-aged White man, went into a Safeway in Houston to pick up a few groceries. After Lambert left the store, a Black man confronted him in the parking lot and demanded his money. Lambert resisted; the assailant pulled out a gun, shot and killed Lambert, and fled.

At the time of these events, Gary Graham was 17 years old, and—having grown up in a broken home in an impoverished, crime-ridden neighborhood—a very troubled individual. Graham admits to having committed several armed robberies around the time that Lambert was murdered, yet from the first claimed to be innocent of Lambert's murder, the crime for which he has been sentenced to die.

There is scant evidence of Graham's guilt. There is, for instance, no solid physical evidence linking Graham to the crime. At trial, it is true, officials did communicate the impression that a .22-caliber handgun in Graham's possession might have been the murder weapon, even though Police Department ballistics tests had in fact shown the contrary. But possession of a supposed murder weapon alone cannot convict, and the case against Graham depends most centrally upon the testimony of a single eyewitness, Bernadine Skillern. Yet official conduct places the reliability of her testimony in doubt as well: Skillern had already been shown Graham's photograph before she viewed the police lineup, a distinction he shared with no other suspect and one that naturally lends itself to false identifications.

Bernadine Skillern, moreover, is not the only eyewitness in the case: There are six more who say they saw the man who killed Bobby Lambert, all of whom claim that Gary Graham could not have been the murderer—Wilma Amos, for instance, who had been shopping inside and was not far behind Lambert on the way out of the Safeway. Amos laid particular stress on a fact all the eyewitnesses—except Skillern—confirm; that Lambert's killer was no taller, and perhaps several inches shorter than 5-foot-6-inch Bobby Lambert himself. At the time of the crime, Gary Graham measured 5 feet 10 inches.

The court never heard the testimony of those six eyewitnesses, not to mention the five alibi witnesses who claim that Graham was with them, miles away from Safeway, at the time of the crime. Their testimony was not heard in the original trial because Graham's court-appointed lawyer did not try to find them. They were turned up by the lawyers working out of the Texas Resource Center. But the attorneys got onto the case a little late—*12 years* too late to make the *30-day* deadline set by the state for post-trial introduction of new evidence.

And so it happens that—despite the legal and political battles fought in his name—Gary Graham was scheduled for execution on June 3, 1993. And so it happens that an ad in his behalf appeared in *The New York Times*, on May 26, an ad featuring a large black and white photograph of Graham's face. It was this face that—as I was preparing for my June 10 departure to Europe—leapt out of my folder to lie next to the color reproduction of *The Lady and the Unicorn,* demanding attention that (despite other pressing business) I could somehow not refuse to give.

Evening had just begun to soften the edges of the May day's clear, sharp light when I arrived at the Mount Saviour Monastery in the hills of Elmira, an hour or so from Ithaca. The founders of the monastery had chosen the spot well: After following the seemingly endless windings of a forest road, I arrived at a spreading checkerboard vista of hill and wood that seemed, all of a sudden, to clarify the twisted sense of the path just traveled, to resolve its shady crookedness (by dint of higher perspective) into a beautiful, calmly ordered design. From the parking lot, I could see—in accord with long-standing Benedictine tradition—a flock of sheep grazing the green flank of a hill. A line of simple, well-kept guesthouses was set out at the foot of the hill, one sign of a less traditional method of tending the flock.

Having come in time for early evening prayers, I entered the chapel. The place was familiar to me, for I had visited it several times within the last year. The advent of my own (for me, quite novel) interest in Christianity a year or so before had coincided with the onset of my involvement in the death penalty. In search of a meaningful connection to the tradition of the religion of forgiveness, I had visited a number of churches in Ithaca but found the services empty, and the inner as well as outer architecture inhospitable to the spirit I was seeking. A friend had told me that Mount Saviour was different, and so—physically, at least—it was. The low-slung stone chapel was simple and austere in its circular design; four sections of rough-hewn wooden pews spread out from a massive stone altar at the center, to the side of which stood a black Giacometti-like sculpture of Jesus. At the periphery of the central section, there stood, a large, beautifully carved wooden harp, as well as the thick trailing ropes from the great bell that sounded atop the chapel. And that was all; the place exuded an archaic, faintly Celtic spirituality.

Just two days before, immediately after learning of Graham's case, I had come to the monastery to gain inspiration for a letter on Graham's behalf: a letter I sent to the White House, and (more pertinently) the governor of Texas, who could if she chose, pardon his life. The place of composition was far from incidental to the letter, for in it I expressed my own sense that the death penalty is incompatible with the tenet of forgiveness central to Christian belief; is, indeed, a desecration of the cross. I was at Mount Savior for the second time within the week on a related mission; I had also initiated an effort to circulate a petition for Graham's life to various religious groups whom I hoped might take the opportunity to express their own spiritually grounded opposition to the death penalty. Having succeeded in gaining the support of Buddhist priests from the Dalai Lama's branch monastery in Ithaca, I was seeking the same sort of support from the Christian community and naturally (albeit naively) thought of Mount Saviour on account of my own connection to the place.

A few strokes on the great brass bell announced the beginning of the service, and I filed into the chapel along with 25 or 30 others. As soon as we were seated, six or eight monks entered from their quarters and began the recitation of biblical passages. After that, several psalms were sung to the accompaniment of the great harp. I had been to services at the monastery before but had never heard the harp played. The music moved me deeply, and, caught up in the spirit of its harmonies, I spontaneously decided to share something of my concerns with the gathering, the group of souls that had, for that little while, been brought so close together by the holy words and music. As the last tone sounded, and the monks were about to file off at the service's end, I stood, saying "Brothers and sisters..." How I would have continued if given the chance, I do not know, for no sooner were the words out of my mouth than the chief monk, a strong-eyed man of 50, cut me off, harshly: "This is not the time..."

According to precept, he was perfectly right. And perhaps the monk who came to me afterward inquiring what it was I had wished to say was also correct in asserting that he and his other Benedictine brothers had left the arena of worldly affairs so far behind, that what happened to Gary Graham was not their concern. It was not my place to tell the monk what was or was not his business; still, I had hoped there would have been room for discussion of the matter, but the monk's resistance to that suggestion was positively stony.

By the time I was ready to leave, night had fallen, and the splendid view I had witnessed upon my arrival lost in the obscure darkness. As I made my way back down the winding, wooded road in the dark, I knew that I would have to travel much farther than Elmira to find a spiritual home—a place that still held the light of the sun, even after dark.

~

A week after my ill-fated expedition to Mount Saviour, several friends joined me at my apartment for a candlelight vigil on the eve of Graham's execution. We intended to watch up to and through the 2:01 a.m. execution time. But late that afternoon, good news came through: A stay had been issued; that night, at least, there was to be no state-sanctioned killing, no fatal jab of a needle deep in the heart of Texas.

This, of course, was grand news, and, yet, when we learned the specifics of the court order later that afternoon, the facts were sobering. The stay of execution was, unfortunately, only a 30-day reprieve, granted in order to allow the courts to decide another pending case before regarding Graham's as closed. The defendant in *Johnson v. Texas* claimed that Texas statute does not allow sufficient consideration of the mitigating factor of youth in capital sentencing.

Since Gary Graham was only 17 at the time of Lambert's murder, a favorable decision in Johnson could conceivably compel reconsideration of Graham's even though the court has previously ruled (in *Graham v. Collins*) that the jury in Graham's trial had not been prevented from giving due weight to the mitigating factor of Graham's youth. The court's temporary stay thus served to reserve the option of review that Graham's execution would clearly foreclose.

After the initial relief, the reality sinks in. The stay is by no means permanent; Graham's life hangs by the thinnest of legal threads. To be sure, the granting of the stay opens a window of hope. His immediate death had been averted, and if the decision in *Johnson* goes the right way, then a new avenue of legal redress may be available. On the other hand, if the ruling in *Johnson* follows the precedent of Graham's own case . . .

That night, we did not call off the vigil: Everything was changed, and yet, at the same time, all was still the same. Nothing essential had been decided, let alone *understood*. Those of us gathered in the room did not have much faith in the court's capacity to achieve the kind of insight requisite for true deliberation on the designs of death. And so we gathered, and so we read—Rilke.

Do not take pride—you who judge—in the dispensable tools of torture, in the absence of rack, neck shackle and chain. No heart is enhanced—not one—because a hint of forced mildness cramps your never tender mouth.

What we've granted the scaffold comes back to us in time, like birthday gifts given children, long ago. Into the pure, high, open door of the heart, he would enter quite differently, the God of true mildness.

He would come in power, like the sweep of the sun, like one divinely charged. More than a wind for the well-insured ships. No less than the soft, secret awareness that silently wins us over within, like a quiet playing child born out of eternal union.

And so it was that when I departed for Paris on June 10—a week after his most recent brush with death—Gary Graham was still alive. Moreover, though hardly out of jeopardy, he would undoubtedly be so upon my return from Europe on July 4. For the time being then, I could, with good conscience, put Graham and the death penalty to the side and turn my attention more fully to the other panel of the diptych that had materialized in the Fine Arts Library—to *The Lady and the Unicorn,* and the whole rich tapestry of Old World culture that still weaves the background of all said and done in the New. On the trail of Rilke's spirit, I hoped to tap the source of literary and spiritual traditions I so treasured, and so perhaps return better equipped to face the challenges waiting me in my native land, in America, death penalty capital of the Western world.

~

Part I

Old World

Dionysus (Louvre)

I

In

the   Rose   Garden

(Window)

Paris/Chartres

6/10 Jardin des Plantes

I arrived in Paris, Orly, around 8 a.m. It was too late to go directly to my friend's; I took the Jetbus to the metro, and the metro to Gare d'Austerlitz to store my luggage for the day. And so without deliberate intent, it was the landscape of the Jardin des Plantes that framed my first view of Paris. Of course, I thought of Emerson—that revelation in the garden when, for a moment, he perceived the unity of forms, and exclaimed (afterward, to himself, in his journal): "I will be a naturalist." The fit of enthusiasm issued in *Nature*, but I am afraid the great man's mind was a little too high-flying for this particular occupation—and, no doubt, a little too impatient of detail, a trifle too youthful to be an *old* master. But it was that kind I had come to seek.

The garden was indeed a memorable place, pregnant with beauty. As I entered the iron gateway, a host of imagery filled my mind, and, for a moment, I thought I saw plants, animals, and people going around in one great ring, appearing and disappearing like members of a brilliant masquerade as if all creation itself were a kind of grand carousel.

Perhaps it is just that, and perhaps man himself runs the show. Or it may be (as the Good Book says) that God stands in for him in that capacity, while man himself is rather a great half-grown child who steps up, pays his penny, and takes his place on the platform of the merry-go-round of time. But the exercise becomes a dizzying affair if enjoyed without intermission. If only our man-child had the sense to step off every once in a while and himself examine the features of his kind before being blurred into oblivion—if only he might paint the faces one can see most clearly just then, when the great carousel first begins to move, for it is then one sees the children's smiles, those perfectly innocent signs of pleasure that are soon mere snatches in the whirlwind—that are all *too* soon swallowed by the speed of revolution, by the unchecked rush of history's man-made mill.

I did not take a photograph of the carousel, since the colors and forms appeared to my mind only, and Olympus did not have a lens concave enough for this trick of vision. But—with a little help from a friend—I did see some other animals in the garden.

THE PANTHER

In the Botanical Garden, Paris

> *The passing of the bars fatigues his gaze*
> *so much, that it can hold no more.*
> *To him, it is as if each bar were a maze*
> *that led to another, and another barred door.*
>
> *The quiet pacing of the strong and supple limbs*
> *that turn around the very smallest sphere*
> *is like a dance of power around the rims*
> *of circles, that hold a great will numb in there.*
>
> *Only seldom does the pupils' curtain slide*
> *soundlessly up—. Then an image enters,*
> *ripples through the tensely stilled stride*
> *and ceases where the rhythm centers.*

~

After my time in the garden, I set out for the nearby Cluny Museum. I passed the great *Pantheon* on the way and made special note of the trio of terms emblazoned on the facade: "Liberty, Equality, Fraternity." These are big words, great words, words that remember revolutionary ideals. Why, I wondered, is the history of hope so beset by betrayal?

In a little square past the Pantheon—*crêpe confiture*. The jam oozed out.

The Cluny was very fine. This medieval museum contained any number of remarkable items: mementos of martyrdom, crosses born by kings, instruments of revenge and revelation, stone heads severed from the facade of Notre Dame. Yet the reason I (and most other visitors) come here has little to do with the more martial side of medieval culture, for I came here to see *The Lady and the Unicorn,* the beautiful tapestry that Rilke describes at the close of Malte's first book.

The Lady and the Unicorn

I spent several hours with the lady and her animal friends, trying to understand the language woven into the fabric of the women and their heraldic world. Calm, light, color, courage, love: all this I could see, but (though I caught some of the words) I could not read the language, find the portal to the frame, enter the mirror of memory hanging on the wall.

This much we know, anyway: The only way to catch a unicorn is to show it its image. And only the Virgin Mary is pure enough for this.

SP II/4

They say this kind of creature never lived.
We weren't told, but allowed to love
the bygone grace of a thing that moved
like the wing-beat of the mourning dove.

Of course it had grown gaunt. Yet while we gazed
soft feet came to feed upon our form,
then—the moment the white head was raised—
light rain fell, stirring up a storm

in your dark eye. How could we stay his flight?
All bindings stop his breath, but blessed night-
shade shares his shape. And so we trust

in what we cannot see, until this crust
rises like the single horn upon his head
and takes us host—alive, or dead.

—Sonnets to Psyche *(adapted from*
Rilke's Sonnets to Orpheus)

6/11   Musée Rodin ⊃ Hotel Biron

Today I visited the Musée Rodin. The museum is located in the old Hotel Biron, where Rilke lived for a number of years. But now the place is mainly Rodin's; belongs to the myriad stones that are the harvest of his hands.

And so I looked and looked, often passing back and forth between the words of the poet (his book on Rodin) and the stones themselves. The old questions recurred: What is the character of Creation; what form of Man, of Woman, of God, is figured in these works? What periods (classic, romantic, modern) hang in the glance and gesture of these forms?

I was particularly moved by two rooms that paid special attention to Psyche and her kin. The forms here seemed peculiarly pregnant, as if a new myth were about to come alive. But other pieces in other rooms, such as *La Main de Dieu,* posed theological problems. Is Rodin's world still that of God the Father; is his artist hand an extension of that masculinism that marks the heritage of our mainstream culture? Here, in this piece, two lovers are cupped in the master, manifestly masculine, hand of the Creator-God. Their act of love, their sex is not the creative act, but is held, contained within a prior genesis.

But part of me belongs to another vision, wants to raise my fist and smash this stone to pieces, because it tells a half-truth or a downright lie. I do not want my image of man, of woman, of creation, to be held within that old, tired hand. It is good for other things (such as justice in the courts of law), but this *issue* . . . well, I would like to put man and woman first, and God second, and make the hand of God over in the image of the act of love.

6/12 St. Chapelle

So today I cross the spreading Seine and visit the Île de la Cité. My thoughts turn first of all to law—to crime and punishment. For the Palais de Justice is here, and I have heard that in these halls even the lawyers wear black robes. The practice portends some confusion, since it seems to mix advocacy and judgment in a most unconscionable manner. But, in the event, I found it not so unfamiliar; in America, too, I have seen prosecutors in robes.

After my brief stint at the Palais, I considered entering the Conciergerie and honoring the memory of the prisoners of the French Revolution. But I was not sure that I could stomach a sortie to the dungeon that had once served as the antechamber to countless executions. We must (or so I told myself), be somewhat selective about the ghosts we choose to entertain in the palace of the imagination and not try to serve too many old masters at once. After all, how did I know M. Paris (as Guillotin's invention had once been called) would not invite me in and smile on me as of old? So I did not stop (just yet) for death, but strode on toward stained glass—the windows in Sainte-Chapelle.

"A bible in color and light" says the guidebook; and so it is. Panel after panel of sacred pictures, frame upon frame of the lore of the Lord adorning the soaring walls; over 1,000 scenes in all. And the colors: blues like the scales of the sea; purples like the cloak of the vine; and golds dug from the treasure of truth.

Looking at the feast, one might well wonder why one should bother to read in black and white, when the religious world is full to the brim with such creative color. Perhaps history would be a quite a different story if books were not largely limited to those colorless negatives which—though filled with light and sound—only reveal their riches when developed by the silver wheel of an adept hand. But this brand of alchemy is not, generally speaking, the province of the priests, who are more anxious to extract doctrine from design than they are to train parishioners how to paint. Who teaches the catechism of color, who illuminates the printed script so the characters might stand out like giant sunflowers in the field of dream?

There were rather too many frames to gain much pleasure from an overall view, and if you go here, I recommend a small pair of binoculars such as those that birders often carry. With the magnifying glass glued to your eye, your gaze is free to wander through the firmament of time, spotting this or that favorite species, resting on this or that ancient olive. The characters of the Flood; the dreams of Daniel; the paintings of the Passion: All these and more appear as so many gems in the kaleidoscope of consciousness, stained glass stones strung and sequenced by the seeing eye.

~

After my bird-watch in Sainte-Chapelle, I proceed across the Île to the grand Notre Dame Cathedral. In the square outside the entrance, I scan the famous facade. It is shorn now, I mean, at least, no longer supporting the weighty visages I viewed in the Cluny, those busts "massacred" in a fit of revolutionary fervor.

Thinking back to the room in the museum, I realize just how eerie it was and how fit an image of history it contained. Angry citizens vent their rage upon the heads of men that are the monuments of established order and sometimes make them *roll*. But does this ever do much more than *shave* man's ugly face, trim the beard that grows so quickly back, so that the revolutionary—who would found another field, and plant seed in some new world-plot—remains history's perennial bondsman, scythe to the same old wiry scenes that spring back, again and again?

This much we can say for certain: History will testify that "great men" are not so easily deposed—even, or especially, when they begin and end in effigy, for heads of stone are far more resilient than those of flesh and blood. Medusa-like, the heads of Notre Dame reappear—not to be sure, in their original station—but in the belly of the museum, the same medieval one that houses the unutterably lambent look of *The Lady and the Unicorn*. Here, the horseless head-men arrest the passer-by with an incontrovertible air, the strange collective stare produced by their condensation in the little room next to the medieval tomb. On the facade of Notre Dame, they were proud, playing sentinel on the public square; but here, the face is filled with a fervent vengeance that catapults out of those unseeing eyes toward the unsuspecting observer who thought she was merely moseying around in an old museum and may never know the sickness that entered her in that dark shaft.

So be warned: Do not look long here; or if you must, come prepared to play the hero, armed—not with a magnifying glass, now, but a *mirror*, so that when your silver sword strikes, you will not merely multiply the monuments of power and add your own heraldic sign to the gallery of gargoyles in history's long hall.

6/13 Parc Rothschild (Boulogne)

Jet lag and the initial rush of images have taken their toll; today I rest in the morning, looking at nothing but the white wall of my friend's Boulogne apartment. But come afternoon, I have enough strength to wander out to Parc Rothschild, a scenic swath of green grass, gorgeous trees, and a little lake with a man-made waterfall where ducks and geese honk their handsome horns. I sit on the bench by the water; behind me, a crew of small French boys plays soccer with surprising skill. I take my pennywhistle out of my pocket and play some tunes. The fowl flock to me; whether for food or love, I shall not say, for I am in France.

6/14 Louvre

The Louvre: what magic attends upon the term—the very name sluices off the tongue like butter down the flank of a French roll. The Louvre: museum of museums. A stranger to its mysteries, I walk the aisle like a bride, wondering who will take me, what manner of man will arrest my wandering gaze, spirit me off to his century, and love me until the walls fall down, and we are all eyes.

(How is it, then, that I still cannot make up my mind about the most important things; whether I am man, or woman, or both in one; if I am flesh and blood, or dry white bone, colored canvas, or marbled stone? If history is eye-scratching sand, or the soft caress of your right hand?)

What can one say—rationally speaking—about this place, this host of history, artifex of the eye?

Guidebooks and signs would have us believe there is *everything* to say about these paintings, these sculptures, these sepulchral stones, and that they have said much of it. But I wonder if our extant word-signs really suffice to say anything at all about the presences that haunt these halls. The citations, situations, settings, and celebratory psalms that collect in catalog and scholarly books—these are but the newsprint and Christian hymnals of history; and tell us next to nothing of—*The Winged Victory of Samothrace.*

The Winged Victory of Samothrace

Victory I ask myself—her. Is that *Victory* to be set up here to be peered and poked at by all those eyes, while after 2,300 years earthmen are no closer to seeing the mystery of her form and still habitually take it for a physical thing? Is it *Victory* to be caught and bound by a race that views vision as a thing of the past and still believes the eyes of our kind sockets soldered in the head? Is it *Victory* to be caged here in this strange aviary, where the tropical birds of time are confined— as if forever—by scientists and citizens who cannot even see the color cascading down the halls like love's laser beams?

> *Where is the man with the right to his possessions?*
> *Who can possess what cannot contain itself,*
> *but only, from time to time, will blissfully*
> *catch itself, then once more throw itself*
> *away, like a child playing with a ball.*
> *As little as the captain can make fast the Nike*
> *stationed on the ship's prow when the secret*
> *lightness of her divine being suddenly*
> *lifts her up into the fresh sea-wind:*
> *so little can one of us call back*
> *the woman who no longer sees us, who*
> *continues along a narrow strand of her being*
> *as if in wonder, and without accident;*
> *unless he felt called and inclined to wrong.*

There are so many people here; so many passers-by, it is difficult even to look at her. How can a suitor pay proper court in a passage thronged by drifting thoughts, by arms and heads and hands that move in a strange sea of motion up and down the stairwell in a seemingly endless ebb and flow? And I myself—how is that, while she has stood here, or there, waiting for me for centuries, I have but a fraction of a day to spend with her, a little hour crowded in betwixt a bevy of other commitments and will hardly be able to look twice before I disappear down the hall, perhaps forever.

This is the way we treat these things, this glorious form. With adulation, yes (even the Greeks set her on a pedestal) but does this display of that original erection, this endless wash of world-wanderers who come, goggle and pass by—can this *begin* to do justice to that indelible beauty? Does it serve her well or allow her to serve us— allow that breathtaking body (no, I am not thinking of the sequestered sex) to inspire the eyes of the slaves in the galley, the motor of our memory, or raise novel west winds that might fill our century's slack white sail? O, that would be *Victory*, indeed, if we might see her in action, breaking waves, giving our titanic craft new, desperately needed directions.

Not, to be sure, with the aim of winning another naval victory, conquering another city. Was she ever really interested in that; could this ever have been her idea of *Victory*? Has not Man always constructed her to serve his own *pyrrhic* ends? What could *Victory* conceivably mean if her art form were not—if she never *could* or *can be*—the *subject* of *history*?

THE WINGED VICTORY OF SAMOTHRACE

A regendered translation of Rilke's "Archaic Torso of Apollo"

> *We never knew her unheard-of head*
> *wherein the eye-apples ripened. Still*
> *her torso glows like a streetlamp, fed*
> *by the gaze that (but turned in) will*
>
> *always hold its fire. Else the surge*
> *of the breast couldn't blind you, or the gentle twist*
> *of the loins reveal the invisible urge*
> *to smile that shudders through Creation's midst.*
>
> *Else this stone would stand deformed and knif-*
> *ed off at the shoulder's steep rock-face*
> *and not ripple like a panther's fluid pelt*
>
> *and not burst through form's constricting belt*
> *like a shining star: for there is no place*
> *that does not see you. You must change your life.*

≈

There is so much in this museum, I do not know which way to turn. So many halls, so many mirrors, so many masters. I feel as if I were a child set down in front of a huge picture book, and have been told to open and read—but when I crack the cover, I find no neat sequence, no satisfying story, but a Prospero-volume full of magic figures (fabled fauns, luminescent lions) that leap off the page and run at me like lost dogs dying to be found, like frames of an unfinished film. And yet it is not hard to see that this is no innocent entertainment, no easy feature made to fit the confined mind of my contemporaries who are, if anything, stranger to me than these figures.

If I am lost here, it is not because I am far from home, but because the windows of my house have all been broken, and I myself am naught but a shivered shard. And yet this homesickness may be labor pain as well, for these estimable ruins are bricks and mortar, glass and glue that only await the journeywork of hands to rise into the flying buttress of a contemporary cathedral. I stand here amid this wilderness of images—an American in Paris—and though a very eccentric pilgrim, am no turncoat, but still a free mason.

∼

Femme et Centaur

Aphrodite de Cnide

The tensed, muscled energy of the bull—meeting? murdering? mating?—the twisted torso of a woman. *Femme et Centaur.* The stark relief of human nature is a fit introduction to this corridor of classical forms, where every curve of the human body is instinct with nature even while the life-lines of the limbs strive toward perfection. It is no accident that the portal to the hall is guarded by the goddess who celebrates the marriage of sense and spirit, the divine form that displays, in gestures of inimitable grace, that these are not two, but one.

Aphrodite, golden goddess of beauty, I almost fear to address you, for what terrible beauty sleeps in this stone, in the syllables of your name. *Sleep,* did I say? When do *you* ever sleep? When has your power ever ceased to rule the earth? Was not Jove himself, when he fashioned the globe, but a child playing with the elements of your form?

Philosophers have tolled the end of religion, but when the sermon grows stiff and cold, the priest still plays with the choirboy behind the pew. The church goes up in arms. But whose rites does this profane? Does not the boy suffer, because the man has suffered—for centuries—the edicts of a faith that has feared and hated you, and always striven to reduce your power to precincts it could control? Nature's beautiful species, all her manifold healers, bear your signature, but the church has always been afraid to love your touch, afraid to read the print of your palms. Your pleasure was never light, or easy; we know your force, but have wholly forgotten the figures of your grace.

And yet, we shall remember and are surely destined to win this religious war. How can it be otherwise? They fight with epistles penned by aging men housed in the ruins of Rome, while you have youth, truth, and Nature on your side. Here, and here, and here are the seeds of this dark rain—do they think they can stop spring from spreading over the face of the earth? They call in vain upon the Father—who has long ago left his house, and the Son—the Son—he does not, cannot, has never hated you, for he is your grandchild.

When the edifice of their faith creaks with age we can no longer bear, your power shall pierce the world like a shaft shot from a golden bow. The masks of god are many, and shape-shift from land to land, but everywhere and always humankind will seek love in the lines of a friend and prophecy in the face of a flower. So one day your rites shall be remembered, and you will have your festivals again—new festivals that shall bend time back on itself until it ties a bow as beautiful as the ribbon that clasps and holds your long dark hair. And then, when someone speaks of "the death of God," the people will look at him as if he were a stranger from another world, an alien from an era they can scarce remember.

I move on down the gallery of lost gods, these beings that are supposed to exist no longer and which the modern mind imagines the fantasy of a youth long since left behind; playthings of a childhood imagination. O yes, we know how to value the pleasures, the wild imaginings of that time; know how to appreciate the delicate work that the eye traced when it believed that it could *see* something other—than itself—and when it saw itself as beautiful, saw its own form as a fit temple of the gods, an abode for divine powers. Yes, we know how to treasure this time; we collect all the pretty toys once fashioned by our hands and set them up in this great dollhouse with names and labels and catalog entries. We do our best to try to remember the childhood, the youth, of the race. But the one thing we will *not* do is take them out of the house and play with them again, for then we might find that we are not so very old as we like to believe and not nearly so big, or "grown up."

Aphrodite, body of beauty; Apollo, your delicate hands at the invisible harp; Dionysius, your slightly parted lips speaking the dream-drama of our lives; no one can convince me you are truly gone. Let them call me crazy—they must believe *you* are so, for I see bars upon the windows, and (if one looks through the side of one's face) the entire place resembles nothing so much as a mental asylum, an institution for those whose strange ailments twist them into striking postures, and send their vision off into the far reaches of space the sane can never enter. It is true, they think you old, infirm, they have locked you up. And yet they think your aberrations interesting enough to put on display and charge all the world to come and look at you—you there—stocked in stone.

And meanwhile, the invisible line of your eyes flies out the window and sprints through the streets to the Pantheon, convening a secret society of new revolutionaries who believe in the saving power of your sense, the melodrama of diseased minds. Deathless gods, spirit me down that city street and tell me how to storm the great bastille that holds you—that holds us—captive. Let my lines swing like a wrecker and free the inmates of the city, for I would be your King of Hearts.

Dionysus behind bars

~

The day at the Louvre has seemed like years (even centuries) though I have recorded but a fraction of what I saw. I must confess, it was, finally, a relief to board the metro and watch French faces disappear into newspapers; to be, once again, a bit of a *bourgeois*. And, especially, to notice the slope of a shoulder, the figure of the girl leaning against the silver center pole.

Do not look too hard at the sketch I did in no time flat, for then you shall surely see that I am certainly no artist and know next to nothing of proportion on the page. Do not look too long, or you will begin to blink and see strange things again—a tree of life growing in the center of the subway, with brands of French apples hanging from the boughs, and names that slip off the tongue like the opening of the alphabet— *Auteil, Boulogne.*

Auteil, Boulogne

Walking home after the ride, I wondered, what colors were her eyes? And if she turned around, and our gazes met, would the windows break, and shatter into stained glass? Would the good citizens on the subway (as they trampled upon us at the next stop) each take a shard or two into their feet, and then later, at night, would the husband stir in his sleep; would he dream, wake and grope in the dark for the switch, desperate to remember, to see—perhaps to paint—the color of his wife's eyes, which he knows now he has not noticed for 10, for 20, for 2,000 years—eyes that he knows now he has never seen or known.

I am back in the Musée Rodin, camera in hand, in the garden. I am looking at women looking at *The Thinker* through their little lens; I am looking at women looking at me looking through my little lens thinking—this is the Gates of . . .

I am at home in this place; yes, I am at home here, have been here for a long, a very long time. How many years ago was it—winter in the city? Now, it is spring again—spring, or early summer, and what was white are red petals fallen at my feet. How I wish my gaze were fixed, as if forever, upon three scarlet drops that might still my wandering gaze. But no, it is far too easy to turn my head, far too easy to prod me on to another thought, another image, another frame that is, still, somehow, always the same . . .

in the
Garden, I am in the Rose . . .
Garden.
Literary Giant Thinking
Citizen with a golden
key
weathered and
worse for
wear.

Idle

everywhere echo and

mirror

seeking of

itself

making a toy of

thought.

one book, one word, one white—

The Gates of Hell

Agape

at the gates of

Hell.

Repeat:

in the Garden. In the Rose
Garden. Literary. Giant. Thinker. Citizen. Outside looking in
through my

eyes

are stained glass
windows

do not

_oo_ at me like
that my love—

confiscate
the camera

feel
the fire

break
this glass

alarm.

~

Let us be precise— let us be
very precise. Report
the facts—nothing more. Leave
nothing out—"the whole
truth," as they
say. For this is
important. There is nothing more—
important. This is
the news, the
story of our kind.

Here— you and I— we're
making history. Here, now. All
the time. So let's be sure—
to get it right. Lives may
depend on it— maybe
ours— certainly, certainly ours.

(They're
shelling Sarajevo again
they're shelling Sara-
jevo they're
shelling Sarajevo again
they're shelling
Sara- jev-

O
Sara

O
Sara

O
dark broken

girl

Repeat: this is the. **Repeat:** There is nothing more … **Repeat.** The President in the
… **Repeat:** Rose. **Repeat** Rose **Repeat** Rose

"So there I was in the. Camera in hand, foot in mouth. Journalist. Pilgrim.
Representative. Man. There I was. I remember it precisely—the Hotel, the old
Hotel Biron. Peaked roof (no fire-watching there); stately stone front, solid as a
lion. Stone walk, too. Not cobbles, exactly, but in that direction. Grey—
the color of rain. And the steps. Three—just three, but long, long as straws. Could
suck the life right out of you if you lingered, if you did not tell

the truth. But before we get to that: on either
side. (Now remember, important. Evidence. What? … happened. what??)
Pallets. That's right—to the right (mine, as I was facing the Hotel, framing
this … picture) some kind of pallets. Stacks of 'em. Piled up there on the right, on
the trolley of a truck. What for? I don't know. They were there. Stacked up.
Waiting. To be unloaded. One by one. Two by two. Fork-lifted … by a man.
What? I don't know. Couldn't lift 'em myself. I just take the pictures, see?
There, on the right, like I said. Grey. Stacked. Horizontals. Looked a bit
like … honeycombs; you know, when they're all dried up—when the bees are
gone, when the comb is paper mache. But heavy. Couldn't lift 'em if I tried.

O.K. Left front, other
side. White. That's right—
white. God knows what—I said God
knows …
White. Not
grey. White. White as … no,
wait. It's spring,
remember? That's
important. This is …
the news. Get it
right, the first
and only

time.

O.K. White . . .

What? Garbage. I said garbage. That's right. I know it's not pretty. Hell, I'm no
aesthete—I tell it like it is. Garbage. White shit. A nice neat pile of crumpled . . .
yeah, scat—like as if that truck (or whatever it is) laid one right there on Rilke's
doorstep. O sweet, pretty—complete
with mirror (see
it there . . .

O.K. O.K. I said, *white* verticals, white . . .

And that was
it. I mean, that was
it—the first

frame anyway

O

I forgot . . .

the windows. O the
windows. O O O

O come on man

come

on . . .

∾

And then *she* was there. Yes, she
was there—at the top of the stair, there
betwixt the lanterns, there
below the
faces
and the

Yes, and then she was ...

1, 2, 3 .... she was

one
woman
two
lanterns (betwixt two
lanterns) **three**
stone faces—beneath three
stone faces, each with a different
look, each with a different
stare. And
the red
and the
white and the

blue no not the American
flag.
Whose I do not know but it is
there, it is
There
in
line with her as she

enters

(WCW where the hell did you ... "Spring
and All" "difficult
news from
poems" all that New
Jersey Jazz ... O
K.O.K.   so I am a
!!modern!! American!! writer!! after
all ... hey, Carlos, go
back to pissing in the
Passaic, will you?

"Watch
your mouth, son, wash
your mouth with
CNNy thing
you say can
be used again
st you—N

ything you say again
st you again
st you a
gain
st
you

again.

~

(At this point in the reading of this poem the reader should hear two
brass bands playing the same tune marching
toward and then past each other.

(My fellow American (scholars) will of course be so good as to inform you—the
vast reading (re)public that the above is a direct reference to the life and works
of Charles Ives, pioneering composer and visionary insurance salesman
who took the social ethic of the business to heart unlike another poet-
salesman who will remain unmentioned
here. But you don't need this
information do you because you
know your founders don't
you what the hell Charlie
Ives loved you and
do you even
know his
name?)

She

is there, is
there and the
flag the red white and
blue flag lies
limp
in line with

her
(again
st you—anything you say may be used
again and again
st you again
and again

and

again.

~

Well, what can a guy say after *that*. Me, I'd been standing at the foot of those steps
for God knows how long cooling my heels and she came along and

click—click—click

high heels and all, just like—

that. Well, I'll be
damned if she didn't open 'im right up, right up like a tin
can—marched right on
through (click—click—click) as if the place were built
for her as if it were her own
home her very own

home.

And the flag—well, see for yourself—there it is, I was

right on the money, wasn't I—Cartier-Bresson

has nothing on me, there it was the ol' red

white and blue happy as a—

there it was the ol'

red

white

and blue stiff

and full—blowing

in the

wind

(any

thing you say ... I

know, doctor, I confess I am

confused—I mean, confused I am

confessed—I know dear

lord I do not

know

what I am

saying and yet

who

knows the form of your

love

better than

(1, 2, 3) you, she and

I?

∾

And that's the truth—the whole and nothing but. I'll swear to every
syllable. Frame me if you want to

see

for yourself; kill

me if you don't want to

touch, to

kiss

my bleeding

face.

(Repeat: This is
important—this is the ...
I SAID THIS IS THE
NEWS. *Read* me I SAID
READ ME do it

now

do

it

write

now

(and never say this isn't the real

thing.

~

Inside the museum, I am magnetically drawn back to the room containing *Psyche and Spring*. There are mirrors everywhere—everywhere mirrors are here, mirrors and windows, windows and mirrors, and the people are inside.

There is the statue of Psyche—smooth white stone emerging from the rock, her head thrown back, tossing her hair. The circumambient sun highlights the body's contours, its hills and hollows; falls lightly on the sex, breast, face and feet. Surely someday this figure will flower, this body give birth.

Psyche has a mirror image, a dark blurred form bent, slightly, with a hand raised, as if to shield herself from the light pouring from the bay behind her. One is so open, unabashed; the other, so folded in. They are sister-subjects, neither one quite free.

Between them stands a girl. She, too, is in the mirror, her back to the black figure and bright light. Her dark hair falls over the dark sweater, both blending with the background figure. Her face is blurred, almost featureless, but one can see it is turned toward the Psyche of the Light, seemingly studying the lines of that form, the long graceful curve that flows from the neck down breast, belly, and knee like a stream over the smoothest of stones.

The girl knows she is the less accomplished of the two. Never has she felt hands move over her like those that shaped that form, never has she been so well-loved. Yet one day, she, too, may be the bride of spring, and the act of her love the silhouette of space, the scripture in the rose window.

Psyche

THE LADY AND THE UNICORN REVISITED

The colors show rich on the cloth—red,
and blue, and green, and the pure white
unicorn. It is not hard to imagine them in-
side the old hotel where Rilke sewed
sestinas of story, his fine print hands
setting in relief the figures of the fold.

The place is strange to us. Within the fold,
life takes on poetic color, and the red
sky is filled with flowers, as if the hands

that stemmed the virgin tide felt the white
cloth a kind of prime, dyed it, and sewed
all sorts of fancy figures in

the swaddling of the sun. Gathered inside, familiar forms reenter the fold
to be redressed, like seedlings sewn
in a revisited field of dreams. Red,
here, does not stop the light, nor does white
contradict color; rather, the hands

that clasp the forgotten flag and the hands
that catch and hold the image in
make a more becoming gesture—white
as bride, not blind, of hue. For the fold
reclaims virgin forest, a plot where red
dress suits a century, as a just-sewn

seam of courage might recall the pattern sewn
on Lincoln's lips when his long hands
limped, and soul was laid in state. Red
has meant so many things; perhaps now, in
here, where past, present and future fold
time together, and the flag (white

red and blue) stars crescive white
moons, the once pilgrim-people that sewed
bales of hate with five fingers folding cruelly on the whip and slave hands
in labor on the loom—perhaps now, in
the medieval mirror raised against the red

sky, in the frolic white feet and gentle hands
that sew another image of beginning in
our reddening eyes, vision may return to the fold.

6 / 17   Chartres

By the 13th century, the art of the stained glass window reached a pinnacle of perfection. At that time, this monumental form-painting became intimately associated with the faces of the church where it was placed, and revealed itself as an original pictorial technique capable of capturing light and shaping it according to its own purposes. The glass window also attained maturity as a mode of religious expression. It became a method of not merely transcribing themes proposed by theology, the history of the church or legends, but a means of transfiguring these themes and integrating them into a previously unrecognized mystic vision.

The monumental Junction of stained glass windows could not be fully established before the beginning of the 13th century—the time of the construction of the Chartres Cathedral—where, for the first time, the prodigious enlargement of the apertures and the extension of the translucent decor assured the glass workers an essential role in fixing the boundaries of interior space—indeed, in the very definition of this space—which became a sort of modeling of colored light.

—Stained Glass Museum, Chartres

Though I was treated well in Paris, it was rather a relief to leave the big city and venture out to the miniature metropolis of Chartres. Narrow, winding ways and windows full of red flowers replaced the sweeping boulevards crammed with cars, and a river with green banks replaced the unapproachable Seine. Yet, for all the charm, there could hardly be any question of "decentering" this small city; now, as in the past, its life revolves ineluctably around the great cathedral that scrapes the sky in the central square, casting the shadow of God's deep designs into every corner of the town. Unacquainted with the spirit of the scene as it must have looked centuries ago, I once more borrowed the lens of my friend.

THE CATHEDRAL

In those little cities, where all around
old houses squat like businesses at a Fair
that beheld it suddenly, and, shockingly aware
shut its booths, and closed without a sound—

its barkers still, its drums broken off
lifting up towards its aroused ears—:
while it, unperturbed in the stiff
old folds of buttressed arrears
stands wholly oblivious of the homes:

in those little cities, you can surmise
how far above the surrounding domes
the cathedrals grew. Their towering rise
covered everything, just as what's wrought
by our own life's far too-great closeness
always surmounts our view, and as if naught
else took place; as if fatefulness
were what piled up in countless feet,
turned to stone, and determined to endure,
not that, which down in the shaded street
takes any name displaying chance allure
and lives in it, as a child might wear
green or red: whatever apron is in stock.
There was birth in this foundation block
and strength and thrust in this soaring rock
and love like bread and wine everywhere,
and portals full of love's provender.
Life tarried in the steady clock
and in the towers that, full of surrender,
suddenly ceased climbing . . . Death was there.

Inside the soaring cathedral, I spent most of my time in my own peculiar form of worship. The statuary, for the most part, left me cold, but the windows were warm with life, the epitome of the place, the heart of its service to the soul. What, after all, is a sacred space but an interior into which the clear light of the sun may pour—not in the pure, unfiltered form which can so readily blast us—but refracted through the shapes and shades of the imagination, the animated annals of the kind. Catechism is caught in creeds; but the passion is in the painting, the colored slides of spirit-life that show whenever the sun shines.

The Museum of Stained Glass near the cathedral went into some detail about the fashioning and care of the precious windows, and—in particular—the ongoing process of restoration. Chartres' windows have been badly dirtied by 800 years of history, and so *we* see the light of the ages through a darkened and a discolored glass—until, that is, we pay a million dollars for a cleaning—*or*, until we take the time to frame our own, and stain the cut-glass walls of our world with the shapes and shades of our psyches, our own imprisoned loves.

The Rose Window

In there, the lazy padding of the paws
creates a stillness, that's almost dizzying;
and how, then, violently, one cat's wandering
gaze retracts suddenly as his claws

into the dark globe's widening dial,
the gaze that, like a lone drifting barque
caught in a whirlpool, swims a while
until it sinks into the center-mark—

when this eye, which only appears to rest
opens, and closes with a deafening roar
tearing deep into the blood-red chest—:

so once the cathedral's stained-glass windows
seized long stooped figures from the floor
and raised . . . the red petals of the rose.

It is true, inside this cathedral, it is difficult not to think about "God"—that great character scrawled so violently across memory's landscape. Many tend to think of "him" as all powerful, and yet I wonder, for isn't his history and the record of his character very much at the mercy of many small human hands? And hasn't it been so ever since the advent of the scribes? Could not one readily see this "God," in fact, as a sort of hostage to history, a kind of captive, a great, powerful heart pacing behind the bars—pacing, back and forth, back and forth, between the black lines of a book, or the grillwork of a window?

And if we look at things this way, many matters appear in a different light. Can we not see, for instance, that if Chartres glass is not *cleaned*, or (still better) broken and *crafted anew*—like some newly dreamed Duchamp—that the church will remain, in part, a bastille of the soul? And what if God (following, perhaps, the cue of his cousins in the Louvre) were to break out; what if——like some great Gulliver rending the tiny ropes tied by tied human hands, or a fallen Titan on the rise—God were to stretch his stiffened limbs and come terribly alive?

GOD IN THE MIDDLE AGES

And they had saved Him up inside their hearts
and they wanted Him to be and rule
and finally hung on him the weighty jewel
(to hinder his ascent to purer parts)

of their great cathedral's massive rock.
And all he was ever now supposed to do
was circle, pointing, while his numbers grew
countless, and give, like some enormous clock,

signs to guide their business day by day.
But suddenly he came fully into gear
and the people of the shocked town

—aghast, because his voice had come so near—
let him run with clockworks hanging down,
and fled before his figures' silent say.

39

And then—as I was rushing out of the cathedral—I saw the angel: the face that redeems time.

L'Ange du Meridien

L'Ange du Meridien

Chartres

In the storm, that batters the strong cathedral
like a heresy contesting heavenly height—
unexpectedly, one feels the more gentle pull
of your laughter, just breaking into light:

smiling angel, tender turnstile
with a mouth made out of a hundred expressions
have you not yet learned how time's confessions
slip slowly off your full sun-dial

on which the day's divisions presently stand
equal sums in Being's deep balance-pan
as if each hour were the sun's whole gold in hand.

Thing of stone, what do you know of our sunlight?
Would you, perhaps, with still more élan
hold your slate out into the night?

∾

The Palace of the Popes

2

Light Shades

Provence 1
Avignon/Orange/Arles

6/18 TGV 863 ⟩ 10:10 a.m. to

AVIGNON—another magic name. As the TGV train races south, I shake the raffle-box of memory for images of my destination. I see Branagh as King Henry rallying his troops behind the lines and wooing the French queen—but after this too modern gloss, my language lapses, and I find no film, no pictures, but only information; unanimated names and dates copied from books of history. I feel like a child studying for a fifth-grade quiz: "the Babylonian Captivity," "1309," "the "second Rome."

The last phrase rings a bell, for this much I know: that the entire region I am visiting takes its name from the sway of the imperial city; I am traveling toward what was once known as the "provinces" of the empire. And so, naturally, I can expect to see ruins: antique theaters, aqueducts, cemeteries that house the sarcophagi of Western civilization. Yet the ancient history of the region is a background for a more colorful present, for Provence is famous for its colors: the blues of the bordering sea, the white of wild ponies, and the yellow—the radiant yellow—of the flowers that mime the sun.

But first there is—Avignon. As I exit the small rail station near the town, I come upon the medieval walls that cloister the city. Walking through the gateway, my imagination jousts with the present day until the latter is, for a moment, unhorsed, and I see ladies in the turrets of the towers, a delicate hand lending a knight a talisman of love.

The victory, however, lasts but an instant, and I soon find that modern-day Avignon is hardly the place for such fantasies, at least in the middle of a June afternoon. The walls appear to be about the only thing that retains much medieval flavor: inside, modern tourist culture has conquered the city. Avignon is a festival town, hosting music and theater events in the summer months, and even now the streets, which are walled by shiny cosmopolitan shops, are packed with people. In a few weeks, the place will be positively besieged. But there is an escape. After checking in at the small but serviceable Hotel du Parc, and shuttering my miniature room against the heat, I make my way to the hill at the top of town, where there is a large garden park—Rocher des Doms—with a fine view of the city itself on one side, and, on the other, the landscape of "The Provinces" and its liquid heart, the River Rhone.

The Rhone is in no rush here and uncoils through the country like a great grey-green snake in spring, a creature not quite awake after a long winter's sleep. Behind the river's winding flank, fathoms of hills unfold, their deep green dotted with the white and orange of the towns and villages hidden in the valleys. On two or three particularly prominent hills, one can even catch a glimpse of a castle, with towers set like white rooks in its corners. As I sit on a bench in the park overlooking the Rhone, crunching my sandwich of crisp white bread and cheese, I muse about the moves made on this nigh Italianate chessboard, the games of love and war played in the hills of Provence. For me, these are the topics of the times.

But for now, there is other business at hand. It is getting on toward early evening, and I wish to visit the city's most imposing edifice before it shuts its gate. And so I wend my way back through the trees and flowers of the Rocher des Doms, pausing briefly to admire the wonderful colors of a peacock (evidently housed on the grounds) that crosses my path. As it spreads its fantail, the feathers display a rainbow of color, and the row of golden eyes wink wisely at me. When the cock closes his fan, I am treated to a gala of setting suns.

Less colorful is the Palace of the Popes, the looming landmark of the Babylonian captivity, when the papacy was moved to Avignon. The place is indeed a palace of sorts, and to term it an imposing edifice scarcely does justice to its scale. The palace, like its predecessor in Rome, looks like a city within a city. And of course, like Avignon, it is a city within walls—great stone walls high enough to cover the sun.

I walk through the arched gateway, and enter the "second city." I traverse labyrinthine passageways, bend through the V-shaped vaults, and pray in cloistered courtyards. I walk through snaking corridors that enter onto enormous chambers (the Grand Tinel): halls as huge as a Viking galley, with woodwork on the ceiling worthy of such a craft. I crawl into cubicles where chalices are held and kneel in the consistory that has seen the canonization of saints. I look at hierophantic portraits of popes, and try to make out the images of famous frescos (the once bright colors faded, the once clear outlines slowly disappearing into the arched interior walls) and slowly, slowly, I begin to remember:

These were the days of that Avignonese Christianity which, a generation earlier, had drawn together round John the Twenty-second with so much involuntary recourse to shelter that at the place of his pontificate, immediately after him, the mass of that palace had arisen, closed and ponderous, like some last body of refuge for the homeless soul of all . . . .

It is a dark, difficult, dramatic place, and I must confess: I do not much like its translation of God's grandeur. I find it hard to feel like a man inside; instead, I sense myself more like a rat in a maze, a subject caught in the corridors of some immense psychological experiment. And as I go gamely on, sniffing for my reward, I begin to wonder at the sanity of the setup; wonder if those who designed this did not suffer some kind of strange delusion; if the science of the church were not a little bit mad. And then I remember the king, who was.

They had accustomed him to spend hours over illustrations and he was content with that; only one thing annoyed him: that in turning the pages one could never keep several pictures in sight and that they were fixed in their folios so that one could not shift them about. Then someone remembered a game of cards that had been quite forgotten, and the king took into favor the person who brought it, so after his own heart were those variegated cardboards that could be separately handled and were full of figures. And while card-playing became the fashion among the courtiers, the king sat in his library and played alone. Just as he now turned up two kings side by side, so the Lord had recently placed him beside the Emperor Wenceslas; sometimes a queen died and then he would lay an ace of hearts upon her that was like a gravestone. It did not astonish him that in this game there were several popes; he set Rome up yonder at the edge of the table, and here, under his right hand, was Avignon. He had no interest in Rome; for some reason or other he pictured it to himself as round and dropped the matter there. But Avignon he knew. And hardly had he thought it, when his memory repeated the high hermetic palace and overtaxed itself He closed his eyes and had to take a deep breath. He feared bad dreams that night.

On the whole, however, it was really a soothing occupation, and they were right in bringing him back to it again and again. Such hours confirmed him in the opinion that he was the king, King Charles the Sixth. This is not to say that he exaggerated himself; he was far from considering himself anything more than one of these pasteboards; but the certitude grew strong in him that he too was a definite card, perhaps a bad one, played in anger, and always losing: but always the same card: but never any other. And yet when a week had passed thus in regular self-confirmation, he would begin to feel a certain tightness inside him. His skin bound him across the forehead and at the back of his neck, as if he suddenly felt his own too distinct contour. No one knew to what temptation he yielded then, when he asked about the Mysteries and could hardly wait for them to begin . . .

So here, even here, inside the twisted intestines of the church, there are those moments when one turns a corner and comes into the open. There was, for instance, the girl—barely visible in the dark cubicle, the profile of her features set like a silhouette in the window, and the whole framed by the austere beauty of a medieval arch. And then when one did debouche into a courtyard, looking up toward the towers and the blue vault of the heavens beyond—it could be that one would catch a glimpse of an angel perched on the parapets, delicately folding and unfolding the wings of desire.

In front of the Palace of the Popes

Finally, I leave the palace; and while skirting the great stone square that fronts it, I am caught by a vignette. A small boy and a girl—a brother and sister—and their dog ply their trade at the foot of the palace stairwell. The boy is grinding an organ and whistling; the dog sits atop the organ, jumps off, scratches. The little girl, with black hair, her pants rolled up just below the knees, stands out in front with a basket. Before them is the great empty plaza; behind them, the imposing, the superimposing, Palace of the Popes.

But there is such infinite distance between them and the tourists across the sea of stone! And—even greater space between them and the palatial edifice of Christianity that is the background of their being.

I begin to make my way across the ocean of stone toward them, taking slow, deliberate steps into the terrible emptiness that surrounds them. I have been traveling in Europe, visiting many museums and churches but now, for the first time, I am a true pilgrim, for it is not any dead God or past master that I approach, but the "still sad music of humanity," the miracle of eternal life. At last, I reach the little girl; she stretches the basket out toward me. It is empty. I plumb my pocket, pick out a piece of bright silver, and drop it into the weave of slatted wood. Her head tilts up toward mine, and a smile opens her face. *"Merci Monsieur."* For a moment, I am my coin, and my coin is a silver fish caught in the flash of the child's mouth.

DEPARTURE OF THE PRODIGAL SON

Now to go away from everything
tangled, that is ours, and yet—not so—
that, like the water in an ancient spring
mirrors us, trembling, disturbing the picture-show;
from all of this—that would continually cling
to us, as if thorned—to part; and leave;
and this and that,
which we no longer perceive
(so familiar is it, so commonplace)
witness suddenly; gently, and with grace
as if from the beginning, and close-up;
and see the impersonal face
of suffering hidden in the too-full cup
of childhood, spilling out upon the land—:
and then, to go, still, hand from hand
as if tearing flesh off the bone
and to go: where? Into the unknown,

far along a warm, unfamiliar strand
that behind each act like some windblown
backdrop remains indifferent: sea, or sand;
and to go: why? Out of instinct, out of urge,
out of impatience; dark expectation's surge,
out of the inability to understand:
To take all of this on and—in vain,
perhaps—let go of what's been learned, to die
alone, knowing nothing of the reason why—
is this the way to make life new again?

6/19 Orange

A few miles off the east bank of the Rhone north of Avignon, Orange, too, occupies a special place in the annals of power, though it was not the church that was the biggest builder, master erector, in this historic place.

If Avignon is called "the second Rome," the city of Orange was founded—and indelibly marked—by the power of the first. Built upon the ruins of a Celtic market, Orange (christened Aurision at its birth in 46 B.C.) was a gift from Caesar to a victorious legion of his vast army, and the entrance to the city bears impressive witness to Rome's military prowess. Arriving here, the traveler encounters no blank rampart, no picturesque medieval wall, but the massive Arc de Triomphe—a tripartite structure standing along the ancient Via Agrippa, the Roman road that once led from Aries to Lyon. Erected in A.D. 26 to commemorate Rome's victory over the Gauls, the stone relief leaves little room for the gentler genres of the historical imagination, but depicts the cold, hard facts of imperial conquest: a host of Gauls falling beneath the gory spears and trampling feet of advancing Roman soldiers. Looking back upon the path of my own first steps in France, I realize, too, that the reach of the Via Agrippa did not end with the demise of the empire; if I had felt so inclined, I could have visited the French emperor's copy of this Roman original, the Arc de Triomphe arching over Paris' own Champs-Elysée. But now, as then, there are more inspiring sights to see.

Near the center of Orange, there is a hill—St. Eutrope—that commands a wide prospect of the distant valley of the Vaucluse. The day is hot, but—never one to miss an overview—I climb the steep, rather rocky slope to the top, where the orange roofs of 12th-century houses, green vineyards, and yellow sunflowers knit a quilt of color for the eye. At first, I imagine I have the place to myself (it is certainly far less peopled than the popular Rocher des Doms) but then, strolling toward the far end of the park, I discover that I am not the only one enjoying the view; am, indeed, by no means its most constant devotee. For here, resting upon a marble pedestal, I find myself in the company of a pure white maiden; one whose eyes seem to me the very windows of this world, and whose hands—delicately opened, as if feeling falling rain—constantly bless it with a gesture of gentle give and take.

But Mary's gaze does not light only upon the natural scene surrounding Orange, for she looks down, too, upon the monumental center of this modern/ancient city, upon the antique site of scenes that have characterized man's most classically grand and dramatically tragic views of himself. Following the line of her gaze down into the huge Théâtre Antique ("the best preserved Roman theatre in France") that lies below, I wonder: Might not the grace of her gaze have cut through the strata of history like a river through a canyon, gradually opening up the hard, rocky, ancient earth to a space of fluid, brand-new birth?

But then I remember: Such labor always imports tremendous pain borne—not by defeated armies—but by the actors who aim to overcome the historic force of man.

It was in the Theatre at Orange. Without really looking up, merely conscious of the rustic fracture that now forms its facade, I had entered by the attendant's little glass door. I found myself among prone column bodies and small mallow shrubs; but they hid from me only for a moment the open shell of the sloping auditorium, which lay there, divided by the afternoon shadow, like a gigantic concave sundial. I advanced quickly toward it. I felt, as I mounted between the rows of seats, how I diminished in these surroundings. A little higher up a few visitors, unequally distributed, were standing about in idle curiosity; their clothes were unpleasantly evident, but their size made them scarcely worth mentioning. For a while they looked at me, wondering at my littleness. That made me turn around.

Oh I was completely unprepared. A play was on. An immense, a superhuman drama was in progress, the drama of that powerful backdrop, the vertical articulation of which appeared, tripartite, resonant with grandeur, annihilating almost, and suddenly measured in its sheer immensity.

I sat down with a shock of amazed pleasure. This which towered before me, with its shadows ordered in the semblance of a face, with the darkness gathered in the mouth of its centre, bounded, up there, by the symmetrically curling hairdress of the cornice: this was the strong, all-covering antique mask, behind which the world condensed into a face. Here, in this great incurved atmosphere of seats, there reigned a life of expectancy, void, absorbent: all happening was yonder: gods and destiny; and thence (when one looked, up high) came lightly, over the wall's rim: the eternal entry of the heavens.

That hour, I realize now, shut me forever out of our theatres. What should I do there? What should I do before a stage on which this wall (the icon-screen of the Russian churches) has been pulled down, because one no longer has the strength to press the action, gas-like, through its hardness, to issue forth in full, heavy oil-drops? Now plays fall in lumps through the holes torn in the coarse sieve of our stages, and collect in heaps and are swept away when we have had enough. It is the same underdone reality that litters our streets and our houses, save that more of it collects there than can be put into one evening.

Antique Theatre, Orange

Let us be honest about it, then; we have no theatre, any more than we have a God: for this, community is needed. Everyone has his own special inspirations and misgivings, and he allows his fellow-man to see as much of them as serves him and suits him. We continually dilute our understanding, so that it may reach, instead of crying out for the wall of a common need, behind which the inscrutable would have time to gather and to brace itself.

6/20 Arles

—the city of shutters. The narrow streets of the city wind twixt the tightly packed houses and hotels, most all of which boast large French windows—airy arches cut in the wall, covered by a colorful pair of (sometimes) slatted wooden boards that swing out into the alleyway when the sun comes up and fold when it falls. The shutters are plain enough—each pair a single hue, without further figuration; but all are different colors. And so, on a good morning, if one is lucky and the timing is right, you can stroll through the street and watch a hundred shades of butterfly wings open and French spirits strive for flight.

The city of shutters, a place of shades: *inside,* or *out?*—that is the question, in Arles. Inside history—the Roman ruins and sarcophagi, or the cloister of St. Trophime—or out on the crowded Place de la République; inside the art—Le Café La Nuit—or out . . . drinking coffee in the street; inside the room (the bedroom, the studio, the sanatorium) or out, in the hot, yellow sun.

Arles, too, has an antique theater. This one is very much smaller and less well-preserved; in fact, only a few columns of the original theater remain. There is an operating stage and rows of seats fanning out from the classical center, but all this is rebuilt and does not produce anything like the impression of the theater in Orange. Though it is pleasant to linger amidst the low ivory-covered walls that still crumble around the border of the theater proper, the truly monumental ruin in Arles is the shell-shaped Roman amphitheater near the center of town. And this very afternoon, a bull game is happening—not the infamous Spanish-style "fight" that ends in ritual murder of the bull—but the sporting, French-style *course libre*. And so—never one to miss a good show—I attend.

You enter through an arch—one of a continuous Doric series—and are swallowed by stone. For a short while, the bright sunlight gives way to damp, cryptic corridors and then— you are there, in the belly of it—this pale grey monster. But still, darkness has lifted; some hungry god has cut open the stomach and left you frighteningly exposed to the unmistakable blue heaven that ceilings the mass of stone.

A few hundred spectators are scattered across the rows of stone that could hold tens of thousands. The figures are dwarfed by the second floor of arches—Corinthian, this time— and the accompanying cornices that frame the stadium against the sky and the row upon row of (largely empty) "seats." The faces are all indistinct, and yet, somehow, an air of anticipation communicates electrically through the crowd. The games are about to begin.

In the holding stall at the far end of the huge arena, the horns of a great black bull are adorned with a cockade; and the object of the sport is the capture of this frail wreath from that dangerous nest. Seven or eight swift young men in white pants and shirts ("*razeteurs*") range themselves loosely round the periphery of the arena. And then the gate is opened, and Coulis, or Romain, or the legendary Amadeus rushes out, horned head held high.

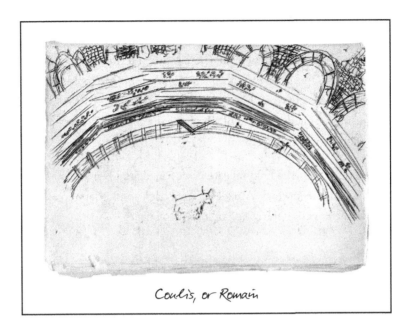

Coulis, or Romain

Standing alone in the center of the huge amphitheater, the bull's strength reigns supreme. Irritated by his recent capture and enclosure, and let out only now in this grassless pasture, he looks about with restless anger and paws the hard, antique earth. Something catches his eye, and—suddenly— he is charging the lithe white form flitting across his field of vision. The spectators—riveted to the rows of stone—draw a collective breath; perhaps he will catch the racing razeteur on the prong of those twisting horns? But Girard, or Ferrand, is always a step or two ahead, and—just when all is about to be lost—leaps to safety over the low wooden wall.

Naturally, this angers the bull even more, and the offending wall feels the force of his rage. Nor is that great strength to be denied; if it were not made to fall conveniently apart at such blows—like Lincoln logs easily reassembled—the wall would be destroyed. The human being may be the quicker creature, but the bull's strength remains undisputed. For the moment, all man can do is play *run, rabbit, run*.

Yet this he can and does do, over and over again, racing past in slanting sallies that draw those small stampedes. Soon the bull is slower, less sure of himself (he cannot catch those white flying machines!) and so, soon, the sprinting *razeteurs* are looking for the tangent to the curve of this tumultuous world, the gesture—perfectly, exquisitely timed— that will lift the leafy cockade from that black brow and win a poet's crown.

And finally, the holding gate is reopened, and Romain, or Coulis, or even the legendary Amadeus, trots back to the dark space from which he issued to the sound of loud applause.

I am staying in the Hotel Gallia, right round the corner from Le Café La Nuit. I remember the picture well, for I have seen it many times before. Not in museums, not in catalogs or history books, not in postcards pulled from distant places like that at which I am now looking to prod my memory as I write. This image is nearer to me than that. I grew up with this frame, for it used to hang on the wall in my parent's bedroom.

They were always fond of art, especially my mother. Her uncle was a painter, a Russian immigrant who studied in Paris and had always kept up with the latest innovations from the Continent. It is easy to see the influence of Cézanne, particularly, on his work, though the modernist vocabulary never broke into the center of his scenes or disturbed the classical strength of his figures: the tailor bent over his worktable, the man bearing the Torah, or (on our wall) the simple, sturdy fisherman mending his nets, his thickset hands playing the mesh like strings of a harp.

I never knew my great-uncle, but his paintings became important to me later in my life. No Van Gogh, his palette was much more muted than the famous Frenchman's, his canvases noted for the fine and infinitely varied shades of grey that inevitably stretched across his skies. His work was rooted in the scenes of his childhood, so very different from those of the brightly lit landscape of Provence. When the son of the Jewish blacksmith in Bobruisk looked up, he would most often see not Mediterranean blue with a huge sunflower in the center but a grey curtain of clouds and rain about to fall.

My uncle's mature work absorbed a great deal of foreign influence without becoming imitative, and he must have owed no little of his strength to his connection with his past, the memories and motifs it supplied him. Never a formalist, his figures, even when they are not specifically religious, have an almost biblical mass, as if the seam of the Old Testament were woven into the tailor's cloth or caught in the tangled mesh of the fisherman's net. He was not merely a painter, but worked in a variety of media: the metalwork that harkened back to his father's smithy, the lithography that echoed his brother's (my grandfather's) photography, and stained glass.

Of all the stories I have heard about my uncle, I recall most vividly the memories of him working after his first heart attack. He was confined to bed then (this being the regular treatment of the condition at the time) and one might have thought the constraining circum-stances would have dampened his will to produce, but the situation seemed to have had the opposite effect on him. It was almost as if his brush with the character of death had opened his own spiritual center; as if that gripping wind had torn open the gates of his heart, so that the love stored there began pouring out all at once, like grain from a too-full silo.

He would spend most of his lying-in time working in his mind—"painting" behind the closed doors of still hands and shut eyes, somewhat like (or so I imagine) that great musician whose ears had been sealed off against the world. And then, when the hour came when he was given leave to rise, he would take up a handful of brushes, and his kingdom's entourage would march across the airy moat betwixt him and the canvas, pouring form, shape and figure forth on the white-cloth world. And then, when all had gone out of him, he would retreat again into the torn tower of his heart, his two hands folded like a drawbridge—or the shut wings of a butterfly—on his once-more quiet chest.

My uncle eventually recovered sufficiently to resume the normal course of his life, but some years later he suffered a second attack. By this time, however, treatment procedure had changed, and—though his health was irrevocably failing—he was allowed freedom of motion. It may be that a wise doctor intuited that this spirit had no wish to take leave of life from a hospital bed and would do much better managing the transition on its own.

And so it happened that my uncle spent the last months of his life doing what he most loved: painting. And these last pictures were quite different from any he had done before; the grey skies were still there, but were shot through with blue and white, as if the sun (so conspicuously absent from all his work) might actually be trying to break through and shine.

Though my uncle had often worked with religious themes, these last paintings did not deal with these; rather, they were all landscapes or seascapes set around Gloucester, Massachusettes, where he had transported himself for this time. And as I think on these things and call to mind the images in those pictures—especially the white triangle in *Fishing Boats*—it occurs to me that I may have inherited, rather than invented, my mode of transport, and heraldic sign. The "father" in the following poem is not him but that of the religious tradition to which he did and did not belong.

White Sail

As a white sail
fills with wind,
so does my mouth
fill with you,
my Father—
your hot breath
drives dueling drafts
over my still smooth skin.

Father—
You are rough
Father—you are gentle—
You confuse me,
Father, and I cannot tell
if you come to slay me
or sleep
along my side.

Whip
me, Father? Paint
my mouth with your
foam, and my craft
is capsized
by your kiss.

Is it because I cannot give myself
wholly to you,
Father—

cannot part my wine-
skin at cold command, spread
my red sea-wings like a sinking swallow

and so come
to bear the bones of wrath?

I am no longer the little
week you once wore
like a bracelet
around your wrist,
for I have grown to treasure
the deep secrets of my
safe, and will not

open

until the fire
burning even now
between us
is set
into a ring
of stone

and given

as a golden

key.

6/21 Arles (continued)

I am in the St. Trophime Church and Cloisters in Arles, on a hot sunny afternoon, writing another letter—this one, to myself.

Read my letter against capital punishment in the Cloisters. One question that arises: Where does help come from to carry out what is here declared? Does it come from the old order of medieval saints remembered here in this sculptured stone, these cloistered courts? Again the same scenes of the Christian mystery—the Annunciation, the Nativity, the Showing of Wounds. But is not a new version of these inscribed in the myth of Psyche and Eros? So why must we worship these old saints

2 - LIGHT SHADES

*and stones. Do they speak? If so, it is through our mouths, our
tears are holy water.*

*From where I am stationed, reading, I see—high above—on
the church "steeple"—the cross; and across the street above the
Place de la République, a bronze statue of MARS carrying a
pennant. The cross, and Mars. Is there a message here? Surely
we do not want another crusade. What is the type of the warrior
that enters the lists in the cause of love? The knight, the spiritual
soldier . . . .*

And *now*, I am in the Musée Ratteau, contemplating *La
Travaille repoussant la Misére.*

*The question is: How will human being reappear after the
fracturing dispersions of Modernism? Do we not need a "new
humanism" on the far side of modernism, a new humanity built
of the mosaic of shattered glass? And to attain this, we need to
break the windows of the cathedral. Only so—only with this
breaking up of the hegemony of biblical narratology—will we
have all our materials at hand.*

The church is not built upon a rock, but upon sand.

And *now* . . . .

I am under the earth, buried in a stone crypt listening to my own
sinking breath. Earlier today, I walked the avenue of marble tombs
in the Alyscamps, once a Roman burial ground and later a famous
medieval Christian cemetery. The stone sepulchres on the avenue all
wore proper caps; as they lined up under the aisle of glorious green trees,
they reminded me of a file of foot soldiers—until I remembered their
house guests had been through that already and that this was a place of
rest. Then, farther on, sarcophagi that had lost their covers found new
uses, serving as baths for blackbirds and cupbearers of the rain.

Alyscamps

Roman Sarcophagi

But what is there to hinder our believing
(the way we're scattered here, like broken plate)
that, for a short while only, thirst and hate
and gross confusion dwells in our receiving

as once in well-adorned sarcophagi
by gems and glasses, by godly figurines
garbed in slowly self-consuming skeins
a slowly dissolved something would lie

until swallowed by the reserved mouths
that never speak. (Where exists the brain
that might serve them, even as they lie?)

Then the ancient aqueducts' stony troughs
steered into them the everlasting rain
that runs in them, waving to the sky.

64

But strolling in the Alyscamp was nothing like being here on the dank dirt in my own cell in the catacombs below the Musée d'Art Chrétien. As the huge Arles amphitheater thrust columns, like stony redwoods, up toward the sky, so the engineers of the Roman underworld sank pillars down toward the center of the earth, as if reaching for the core, and hollowed out a huge subterranean city, a nigh Egyptian morgue. And I am here, crouched like a thief inside that "public housing," the pale light I switched on upon entering faint as a heart about to stop. What if it should go out? Where would I be if the body's eye closed?

THE PRISONER

My hand still has just one
gesture for fending off;
dampness falls on stones
ancient, and hewn rough.

I hear only this knocking
and my heart beats along
with the water's tick-tocking
and loses its song.

If only the tap were tighter,
an animal might come, or go.
Somewhere it was lighter—.
But what do we know.

They say the habits we contract in life follow us to the grave; that, for instance, persons who loved to greet the sun early in the morning—that their corpses will be what are called "early risers," and that you can hear their voices in the throats of birds.

That is how you lost, always:
never as one in possession: but, like a dying person, who,
bending into the damp gusts of a March evening loses
the springtime—alas—in the throats of the birds.
Far too much you belong to grief. If you could forget
the least of those forms whose pain is beyond measure,
you would call down, shouting, hoping they were still curious,
one of the Angels, its darkened countenance incapable
of sorrow, yet straining again and again to describe
to you, how you wept for her, that time, long ago.
Angel, what was it like? And he would imitate you and not
comprehend that it was pain, as one calls after a calling bird,
mimicking the innocent voice that fills its throat.

Daniel, Musée d'Art Chrétien

Sepulchre, Musée d'Art Chrétien

I come up out of the underground. I wander bewildered amongst the stone sepulchres kept on the main floor of the museum. Unlike the bare crypts below, these were beautifully sculpted, the walls covered with fine bas-reliefs of religious figures, tableaus of sacred time.

Half-mechanically, I take out my camera, and as I do, the sun streams through the half-broken windows of the building, shedding a pale yellow light on the faces of figures. My dumb cyclops eye follows the path of the sun, and—like a dark dial at dawn—seeks to record the progression of the spiritual hours etched in stone. Greek and Roman heroes, the framers and prophets of Old Testament Law, the bearers of the New. And what is this? A new kind of red, white, and blue showing up on the sun-dial, the "angel of the book" making annunciation of the spirit of the age.

But (is it not always so?) the vision is written in a language we cannot read.

Angel, Musée d'Art Chrétien

The Angel

With a tilt of the brow he will reject
everything that limits, or might bind;
for through his heart moves majestic and erect
the eternal advent of the divine mind.

The heavens stand before him, full of forms,
with each calling to him: come, know me.
Give none of your heavy charge into his free
and weightless hands. Then he'll come in storms

at night, and try you with a wrestler's hold,
and rage like angry pillage through your home
and seize you, as if he'd made you out of loam
and break you out of your too-human mold.

≈

Waterwheel on the river Sorgue

3

On Foot to

the Fount

Provence 11
Les Baux/Camargue/Aix/Vaucluse

6/22 Les Baux

Magnificent landscape in Provence, a land of shepherds, even today still imprinted with the remains of the castles built by the princes of Les Baux, a noble family of prodigious bravery, famous in the 14th and 15th centuries for the splendor and strength of its men and the beauty of its women. As far as the princes of Les Baux are concerned, one might well say that a petrified time outlasts this family. Its existence is, as it were, petrified in the harsh, silver-gray landscape into which the unheard of castles have crumbled. This landscape, near Arles, is an unforgettable drama of Nature: a hill, ruins, and village, abandoned, entirely turned to rock again with all its houses and fragments of houses. Far around, pasture . . .

—Rilke

The bus is winding up what appears to be a miniature mountain capped by a fortress; as one comes closer, one sees a village nested amongst the rocks. For a moment, I am reminded of vaguely similar scenes from the American Southwest: pueblos perched, like eagle's nests, on ledges; cliff dwellings accessible only by ladder in the Canyon de Chelly.

But as soon as one arrives, the comparison fades, because the once-abandoned little town has been resuscitated and succumbed to the disease of tourism. And yet, the local museum does display a variety of things (manuscripts, maps, coats of arms) that illustrates the strange and potent mixture of the sacred and profane that characterizes the contradictory history of this place.

. . . Like most Provencal families, the princes of Les Baux were superstitious gentlemen. Their rise had been immense, their good fortune measureless, their wealth beyond compare. The daughters

73

of this family walked about like goddesses and nymphs, the men were turbulent demigods. From their battles they brought back not only treasures and slaves, but the most unbelievable crowns; they called themselves, by the way, "Emperors of Jerusalem." But in their coat-of-arms sat the worm of contradiction: to those who believe in the power of the number seven, "sixteen" appears the most dangerous counter number, and the lords of Les Baux bore in their coat-of-arms the 16-rayed star (the star that led the three kings from the East and the shepherds to the manger in Bethlehem: for they believed that the family originated from the holy king Balthazar). The "good fortune" of this family was a struggle of the holy number "7" (they possessed cities, villages, and convents always in sevens) against the "16" rays of their coat-of-arms. And the seven succumbed.

Leaving the *centre ville,* I climb to the bare plateau at the crest of the hill, which commands a panoramic prospect of variegated land around. The sky is cast over, and the grey somber mist provides a dramatic backdrop for the scene behind the village, the eerie Val d'Enfer. Dante had a vision of Hell here; they say that the craggy rocks that rise behind the village like some demonic Zion provided inspiration for his *Inferno.* And here, as so often happens, history seems to unfold the fate signified in the lineaments of the land.

These warriors (the Princes of Les Baux) reigned over the destiny of Baux and their 79 fiefs for five centuries. These proud and rebellious Lords, allied with the great families of Europe, fought against their powerful neighbors of Toulouse and Provence and against the realm of France which was progressively encircling Baux. These ceaseless conflicts devastated Provence, reducing it to a theatre of violence, looting and fires.

Out of these troubled times emerge certain emblematic figures, among which were Hugues I, founder of the first fortress, Raymond des Baux, who led the Baussenques wars, Barral, Raymond de Turenne named "the curse of Provence" who threw

his prisoners from the top of the castle, and finally Alix des Baux,
last of this unruly stock.

Yet this violent history is by no means the sole legacy of
passionate *Les Baux,* for it seems this site is, above all, a study
in contrast, and a meeting of extremes. And so: while the God
of war indubitably held the region in his iron grip, his heavenly
consort was no less active, and so lent quite another side to the
history of Les Baux:

Yet it is also in Baux that "courtly love" was practiced by
well-renowned courts. In the latter, poets and minstrels gathered
around the gracious young ladies of the house of Baux: Baussette,
Doulce, Phanette, Huguette, Clairette, Azalais and Passerose
were sung of by the troubadours and became famous throughout
Provence.

When Alix died, Baux joined the house of the Counts of
Provence and became a Barony. Good King Rene and especially
his wife, Queen Jeanne de Provence, enabled the village to live
a new period of wealth: mansions and magnificent residences
were built on the rock and contributed to embellishing it.

While the character of Les Baux is stamped, above all, by the
medieval heritage represented by the Saracen and Paravelle towers
(the remains of the 10th century citadel that crowns the lookout of Les
Baux), the geography of the site is astonishingly complex and multi-
layered. There are traces of prehistoric periods in the rocky grottoes;
a monument to Charles Rieu, a peasant poet who authored Provencal
song and a translation of the *Odyssey*; and a cemetery where modern
poets and painters rest. There is also an old windmill near a rainwater
reservoir, a pigeonry dating back to the 13th century; a 16th-century
Romanesque chapel dedicated to Saint Catherine. The view of the
Val d'enfer (Hell's Valley); on the one side is complemented by the
Vallon de La Fontaine (the Fountain Vale) on the other. If one is
poetically inclined, one can find traces or prefigurations of most

anybody here, in this paradoxical palimpsest, this "magical haven in the clouds."

It begins to rain. I retreat into a grotto that commands a view of the valley and take out the book I brought along for the occasion: the epical adventures of William d'Orange, as recounted by Guillaume. The hero seemed a most suitable subject, not only because he hailed from the region, but also because Dante thought highly enough of him to place him in the sphere of Crusaders besides Charlemagne and Godfrey of Boulogne.

As I read in rhythm with the soft beating of the drops on the roof of the grotto, William performs deeds in service of his God. And yet, for all his devotion, good William did seem rather unremittingly martial, and I wondered if he too might not have finally been beaten by his own warlike ways. I finally set the book aside, and, peering out into the mist-shrouded rocks veiling the Valley of Hell, dreamed of other, more familiar figures, perhaps catching a fleeting glimpse of one who could easily have stepped forth from William's book, though this sketch of him is drawn from the records of "good king René":

Not until then, not until his years as a shepherd, was there any peace in his crowded past. What art is broad enough to simultaneously evoke his thin, cloaked form and the vast spaciousness of his gigantic nights?

This was the time which began with his feeling as general and anonymous as a slowly recovering convalescent. He didn't love anything, unless it could be said that he loved existing. The humble love that his sheep felt for him was no burden; like sunlight falling through clouds, it dispersed around him and softly shimmered upon the meadows. On the innocent trail of their hunger, he walked silently over the pastures of the world. Strangers saw him on the Acropolis; for many years, perhaps, he was one of the shepherds in Les Baux, and saw petrified time outlast that lofty race which with all the conquests of seven and *three, could not get the better of the sixteen rays of its own star. Or should I imagine him at Orange, resting against the rustic triumphal arch? Should I see him in the soul inhabited shade of Alyscamps, where, among the tombs that lie open as the tombs of the resurrected, his glance chased a dragonfly?*

It doesn't matter. I see more than him: I see his whole existence, which was then beginning its long love toward God, that silent work undertaken without thought of ever reaching its goal. For though he had wanted to hold himself back for ever, he was now once again overcome by the growing urgency of his heart. And this time he hoped to be answered.

~

6/25 Les Saintes-Maries-de-la-Mer (Camargue)

Nature calls. No artist, no pilgrim, no person of color could come this close, and not yearn to witness Mediterranean blue. The coastline here is not defined by the rich and famous (like Nice and Cannes), but by the spreading marsh grass and spectacular wildlife of the Camargue, a wedge-shaped region between Arles and the coast.

As the bus rolls south from Arles, we leave verdant hills behind. The land flattens out, and the dominant deep green gives way to the tan of the sand-colored earth, to waves of straw colored grass. And then, when at last one arrives at the little city that is the gateway to the sea and walks through—all of a sudden the world is orange, white, and blue, blue, blue.

Orange for the tile rooftops of Les Saintes-Maries-de-la-Mer, a town rich with biblical legend and Gypsy lore, and site of a ritual that marks the crossroads of both. The place derives its name from not one but *three* Marys: Mary Magdalene; Mary, mother of the apostles John and James; and Mary, sister of the Virgin, all of whom are said to have landed here in A.D. 40 upon fleeing persecution in Palestine. It is also said that the three Marys sailed in the company of the risen Lazarus and their Egyptian servant, Sarah, patron saint of the Gypsies. The town is thus a historical center for gypsy people, and I was taken with the Gypsy symbol I discovered in a jewelry store: a small stick figure with outstretched arms supporting the arc of a rainbow overhead.

But a glyph is but a glyph, and I found another bit of Gypsy symbolism still more compelling. Every year, toward the end of May, nomadic individuals from all over Europe come to celebrate the annual Pèlerinage des Gitans (Pilgrimage of the Gypsies) when, amidst the strewing of flowers, they bear Sarah from the crypt of the church down to the Mediterranean. Thus myth, history, and ritual all bear witness to the deep relation between the life of the Traveler, the origins of Christianity, and the bottom of the deep blue Sea.

White for the astonishing sand that stretches for miles and miles along the coast. The sweep of the beach toward the horizon, the clean lines reaching toward infinity, call to mind the mystic reach of an abstract expressionist painting (a Newman zip perhaps) but there is nothing abstract about the feel of my feet on the sand. The shore is littered with multicolored shells, and, as I stroll along, I collect different kinds like beads for a necklace that someday may, like an abacus of analysis, help me retrace my path. Nor am I above getting a little wet or building my own miniature castles, though of course these cannot compare with the imposing fortress at Les Baux. The shore is a place of mythic beginnings; the magic zipper of land, sea, and sky that—like a shot from Eros' bow—opens the world to the soft silver lap of love.

Blue for the sea itself, the magic Mediterranean. Blue, to *begin* with—but only that, for, if the truth be known, there is really no end to the colors one can find in the sea. Much too deep to be identified with a single shade, the sea often seems to change before your very eyes, though you could never tell exactly when or how or why with even the most precise instrument. What one witnesses here is motion without measure, as if the now gentle waves contained, in their fathomless action, the very idea of interval, the principle of appearance per se.

Sometimes I think the world would be a very different place if philosophers and religionists were required to submit their designs on love and truth to the test of Nature. Should not the priest who would preach the laws of the heart know the colors of that eternal fountain? If you wish to learn humility, don't—for heaven's sake—abuse your beautiful body; take a palette and a brush, go out and try to paint the sea. It will be best to choose a time when a storm is coming in, for then the color fields will have separated a bit. And remember: The one who would ride the eye of a hurricane has no need to stir.

But today there are no storms on the horizon, and there are other natural beauties to observe. The charismatic color of the Camargue is not only element, but animal as well; the white of the strand is echoed in the striking wild ponies the Spanish herdsmen still ride through the marshlands of the Camargue. Sometimes they are herding the coal-black bulls that also run free in the marshland—the same stout fighters that star in the *cours libre*. And, as if that animated interaction of black and white were not colorful enough, Nature has spilled striking pink over the canvas of the Camargue. Flamingos stand stiff-legged in the marsh—sometimes single, sometimes in flocks of a hundred or a thousand—enough, at any rate, to mock sunset when they lift and fly.

Flamingo

Walking here—along the beach, or the trails through the marsh just inland—surrounded by sea, grass, sky, and pink flamingos, it is not so hard, after all, to lift the curtain of history, to go behind the puny imagination of man, and stand once more at the origin of things. Surely, every being that strolls this strand can bear true witness to the possibility—yea, the *necessity*—of beginning again; anyone, that is, who does not play the ostrich; does not stick her head in some great book so as not to have to believe her eyes. True, the beauty can be blinding—and that is why if you come to see the flamingos in flight, you should take a good glass along, almost as if you had come to witness the eclipse of the sun. Then, walking back to the town in evening after the spectacle, you can report the "miracle" in good faith.

Long walk today around Les Saintes-Maries and the Camargue, 25 kilometers or so, to the lighthouse and beyond. On the way back, walking back toward Les Saintes-Maries, the orange rooftops painted against the fading blue above blue sea, my mind wandered back to early Christian times, for the life of Christ played itself out across these waters. From this vantage on the shore, Les Saintes-Maries reminds me of a holy city, a place of pilgrimage, a "new Jerusalem."

"Early Christian times"—that time when the life of Christ was first interpreted, and, eventually, certain interpretations established, codified into doctrine, the creed of the church. But what did Jesus teach?

That night, in a little white-walled room, I read and reread *The Gospel According to Jesus,* another slim paper in red, white, and blue:

And he went again to the lakeside, and began to teach, and so many people gathered that he had to get into a boat on the lake. And he sat in it, and the whole crowd sat on the shore, up to the water's edge.

And he taught them many things in parables, and said, "What is the kingdom of God like? It is like a man who sows a seed on the earth: he goes about his business, and day by day the seed sprouts and grows, he doesn't know how. The earth bears fruit by itself, first the stalk, then the ear, then the full grain in the ear. And when the grain is ripe, the man goes in with his sickle, because it is harvest time.

"The kingdom of God is like a mustard seed, which is smaller than any other seed; but when it is sown, it grows up and becomes the largest of shrubs, and puts forth large branches, so that the birds of the sky are able to make their nests in its shade.

"The kingdom of God is like a treasure buried in a field, which a man found and buried again; then in his joy he goes and sells everything he has and buys that field.

"Or the kingdom of God is like this: there was a merchant looking for fine pearls, who found one pearl of great price, and went and sold everything he had and bought it.

"Thus, every scribe who has been trained for the kingdom of God is like a householder who can bring forth out of his treasure room both the new and the old."

And someone asked him, "When will the kingdom of God come?"

And he said, "The kingdom of God will not come if you watch for it. Nor will anyone be able to say, 'It is here' or 'It is there.' For the kingdom of God is within you."

After reading, just before sleep, I take a late night walk by the sea. The moon is up, the stars out, and a soft wind blows the whispered words of a distant friend into my open ear.

SONG OF THE SEA

Age-old breath from the sea,
sea wind by night:
*   blown for no one;*
if we awake, two
must go through
how to endure you:
*   Age-old breath from the sea*
blown

as if only for milk-stone,
pure space
torn off of a star—

O how the fig-leaf's love
feels you
in the moon above.

6/26 Les Saintes-Maire/Arles

The next day, I spend much like the last, though my feet tell me I need not walk quite so far. Tonight, then, I am in Arles (a way station now) one last time and pen these words to a friend:

Dear A:

I write to you from a small hotel room, in Arles. These rooms are one of the great drawbacks of traveling, at least for one in my income bracket. They are, almost without exception, drab if not downright depressing affairs. And it is so hard to feel "at home" in them. For most people, perhaps, this would not be too terribly important, but I am so keyed into interior space (I __am__ an interior space!) that it wears on me, and makes it difficult to __write__—which wears on me even more. For I inevitably begin to feel like a stranger to myself if I do not write for a few days. Like some stringed instrument, my psyche goes out of tune . . . .

So I do what I can to make a space of my own, even when I am here, a long way from "home." There is a small desk in my room (I do not let rooms that do not have at least that!), and it is now adorned with a few things that give me some small comfort. In the right hand corner, a postcard of Van Gogh's "Le Café La Nuit," stars shining in the black sky—the "real thing" is just around the corner. Next to this, a sprig of sage, that pungent delicious odor, the little bunch of sharp chartreuse that looks so much like a small tree or a miniature mind; and then, best of all, spread out in front of these, the treasure brought home from the sea. Twenty-five beautiful shells of varied shapes, sizes, and colors, a veritable orchestra of innuendo. Long fluted purple fingers that look for all the world like pieces of organ pipe, scalloped semicircles that curve like the bell of a horn, drab black mollusks opening their mouths and . . . my two special treasures, of which I cannot speak, for they are secrets, magic things that cannot be told, but only shown.

And isn't life—I mean our real life—like that: something so deep, so unfathomable, that we can hardly begin to say what we are. Of course we have our shallows, the moments easily and casually exchanged, the waters we wade through without much of a wetting. And perhaps this is where most so-called society spends its time at the beach, seldom bothering, in fact, to notice the inestimable beauty of the shells washed up on shore, too busy to wonder into questions about the place from which they came, the origin of that unseen depth from which all life arises . . . .

Thank you for being a good friend before I left, for sharing a little genuine humanity—we might even say "love," which does not always come in red, but, like the shells on the shore, comes in all kinds of shapes, sizes, and hues; an endless variety. Why does human life—our capacity for caring and sharing—seem so poor and cramped so much of the time when Nature is so rich, when there is so much of us to give and take? Ah, but we are directed to forget all that, to forget the shore from which we come, each and every one of us a special brand of beauty, another scallop in Aphrodite's shell.

SP II/1

Breathe, invisible poem!
The darkness of the world
grows round you like a home
made pearl, or fallen flag unfurled.

One and only wave
whose slow sea I am
why should we not save
space for singing in?

How many of these rooms were done
in my new shell? These stones
wound like my lost son.

Children, do you know me? You who bear
my beauty in this box of bones?
Do you love each other, or your fear?

◦∼◦

6/27 Aix-en-Provence

Cours Mirabeau, the central thoroughfare in Aix, has been called "the most handsome street in France." The trees that arch over the busy avenue are magnificent, but the buildings seem to me uninspired, and the street paved with people; wall-to-wall sidewalk café. I am glad to leave this street and begin what I am really here for: following in the footsteps of Paul Cézanne.

That *is* possible here, quite literally. For while Rilke may have had only forms and shades to go by in his quest to understand the spirit of the artist who (after Rodin) taught him most, the city of Aix has thoughtfully lent the quest for Cézanne a more physiobiographical form: a trail of bronze footsteps, inlaid in its streets and walks, which lead one, step by step, to many of the places significant to the painter: his birthplace, the cathedral at which he worshipped, the studio he left (an unfinished canvas on the easel) at his death in 1906.

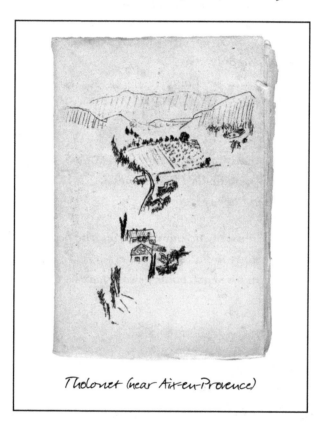

Tholonet (near Aix-en-Provence)

It would be foolish to look at the path as a yellow brick road to the spirit of the master; nonetheless, it is a useful mnemonic device, especially for those who, like myself, may be considering a kind of discipleship; debating just how they may wish to play the role of the sorcerer's apprentice. As I follow the bronze markers, eyes trained upon feet moving in tandem, I am set to thinking about religion again and how it went off-track the moment the warm words of the Son were made—not the *prism,* but *prison*—of God. Anyone who follows in the footstep of a real master will at some point turn a decisive corner and come face to face with the truth that *regard* for the divine can never be a matter of collective opinion; as if the goods of the spirit could be purchased at some Safeway every Sunday morning. But the lifework of the artist is inherently religious: It is the way of the pilgrim, the pathfinder whose work is a rose found amidst a bramble of thorn.

. . . today I wanted to tell you a little about Cézanne. With regard to his work habits, he claimed to have lived as a Bohemian until his fortieth year. Only then, through his acquaintance with Pissarro, did he develop a taste for work. But then to such an extent that for the next thirty years he did nothing but work. Actually without joy, it seems, in a constant rage, in conflict with every single one of his paintings, none of which seemed to achieve what he considered to be the most indispensable thing. La realisation, he called it, and he found it in the Venetians whom he had seen over and over again in the Louvre and to whom he had given his unreserved recognition. To achieve the conviction and substantiality of things, a reality intensified and potentiated to the point of indestructibility by his experience of the object, this seemed to him to be the purpose of his innermost work; old, sick, exhausted every evening to the edge of collapse by the regular course of the day's work . . . hoping nevertheless from day to day that he might reach that achievement which he felt was the only thing that mattered. And all the while . . . he exacerbated the difficulty of his work in the most willful manner. While painting a landscape or a still life, he would conscientiously persevere in front of the object, but approach it only by very complicated detours. Beginning with the darkest tones, he would cover their depth with a layer of color that led a little beyond them and keep going, expanding outward from color to color, until gradually he reached another, contrasting pictorial element, where, beginning at a new center, he would proceed in a similar way. I think there was a conflict, a mutual struggle between the two procedures of, first, looking and confidently receiving, and then of appropriating and making personal use

of what has been received; that the two, perhaps as a result of becoming conscious, would immediately start opposing each other, talking out loud, as it were, and go on perpetually interrupting and contradicting each other. And the old man endured their discord, ran back and forth in his studio, which was badly lit because the builder had not found it necessary to pay attention to this strange old bird whom the people of Aix had agreed not to take seriously. He ran back and forth in his studio with green apples scattered about, or went out into his garden in despair and sat. And before him lay the small town, unsuspecting, with its cathedral; a town for decent and modest burghers, while he—just as his father, who was a hat maker, had foreseen—had become different . . . .

Surely all art is the result of one's having been in danger, of having gone through an experience all the way to the end . . . The further one goes, the more private, the more personal, the more singular an experience becomes, and the thing one is making is, finally, the necessary, irrepressible, and, as nearly as possible, definitive utterance of this singularity . . . Therein lies the enormous aid the work of art brings to the life of the one who must make it: that it is his epitome; the knot in the rosary at which his life recites a prayer, the ever-returning proof to himself of his unity and genuineness, which presents itself only to him while appearing anonymous to the outside, nameless, existing merely as necessity, as reality, as being.

I had no time to follow the Chemin de Cézanne to its end—with the afternoon waning, I had to choose between a visit to Cézanne's studio or Musée Granet, which held four of his works in its collection. I chose the latter and spent my last afternoon hours contemplating color *a la* Cézanne, and reflecting yet again about what we rather casually call art, and (still more carelessly) religion. For it seems to me very vain to pretend to say anything of "God" until one has learned to *make* something of nature; that in fact what we are truly given to know of the divine is very near to us—is housed, like a special guest, in the shapes and shades of things themselves. We presume a picture of a blue vase, or a poem of red roses, is not religious scripture because it does not mention "God" by name, or impress us with moral demand, but only quietly, namelessly, solicits our love. Our theology empties the world of beauty; nor does the canon of "family values" save sacred space for a letter to a friend:

Dear J:

I write from a quite fine hotel room in Aix-en-Provence, dwelling and workplace of Paul Cézanne. Have I ever mentioned the small book Letters on Cézanne *to you? A collection of Rilke's letters to his wife, Clara, dealing primarily with the work of this great artist who, after Rodin, counts as the most significant "influence" (at least as far as the visual arts are concerned) upon Rilke's work. It was his engagements with Rodin and Cézanne— the character of concreteness, of objective realty—encountered in their work and (just as importantly) embodied in their patient labor that led Rilke forth to one of his first great achievements as a poet—the* Neue Gedichte (New Poems) *of 1907 and 1908.*

*It is above all, I think, these poems that figure as the counter-part of my trip to date. Of Rilke's best known works (*New Poems, The Notebooks of Malte Laurids Brigge, Duino Elegies, *and the* Sonnets to Orpheus*), it is, interestingly enough, these that have so far been least accessible to me. And, over the course of the last several weeks, I have discovered why: these lyric poems are deeply rooted in the things about which they speak, for they are really naught but mouthpieces for these things—and many of them belong to a world that is, perhaps, difficult to enter unless one actually encounters the things themselves, and can feel the history of which they are a part (even if only residually, detachedly, like flotsam and jetsam from the wreck of history). The Roman sarcophagus, the medieval cathedral, the angel with the sundial on the facade of Chartres; how much it helps actually to see these things! For then the spirit of Rilke's writing is conducted much* more confidently down the corridor of years, and poured more surely into us; the substance of these things still contains—and helps us contain— the inspiration that gave rise to the poetry. And then how much more surely do we see the world this writing participates, and recreates; finally, we have the <u>background</u> against which the figures of Rilke's poems stand out.

I, of course, am an advocate for the power of imagination, and yet, any artist would be loath to deny just how formative actual sense experience may be for our vision. The natural order of creation is: from eye to hand to mouth; impression, labor, utterance. But how strange it is that I, so intellectual a poet, often put the hand before the eye, so that my eyes are not in my head, but are rings upon my fingers . . . .

Well, I am afraid this is a very uninformative letter. I am sure you want to hear more about this trip. It has been very rich; I cannot believe it is almost over, for it seems it has just begun. We must be careful lest life feel like that; I mean, I do not think we want to come to our seventieth or eightieth year, that time when we know the terminal is just round the corner, and have the feeling that—had we known or dared a little more—that our life would have been 10 or 100 times deeper than we had lived it; that we had spent a whole lifetime getting the hang of reading the menu, learning the bits and pieces of language—just enough to get by, but never touched the core of our course, never read or written the poem that gives the principle of our place on earth, the scripture of our soul.

THE BOWL OF ROSES

You saw the spark of anger, saw two boys
roll themselves into a ball of something
that was hate, writhing upon the earth
like a creature set upon by swarming bees;
stage-actors, towering anti-heros,

crazed horses clashing and crashing down,
wild eyes casting about and baring their teeth
as if mouths were the peeling back of skulls.

But now you know, how all that is forgotten:
because before you stands the bowl of roses,
the flowers filling the unforgettable vase
with that extremity of being and of bending,
enduring never-giving-out, existing
that could be ours: our extremity, as well.

Silent life, opening without end,
using room without taking room away
from the room neighboring things diminish,
being almost limitless as pure inwardness
saved and set aside, rare tenderness
and self-luminosity, right up to the edge:
is there anything we know like this?

And then like this: that a feeling arises
because flower petals touch flower petals?
And this: that one opens like a lid
and below lie only eyelids, closed,
as if they, wrapped in dark slumber
had to damp the power of inner vision.

And above all, this: that through these petals
light must pass. From a thousand heavens
they slowly filter that drop of darkness
in whose fiery glow the confused bundle
of stamens rouse themselves, and begin to rise.

And the movement in the roses, see:
gestures with such small angles of deflection,
that they'd remain invisible if their rays
didn't spread like the sun's through the cosmos.

See that white one, that opened blissfully
and stands there in the great unfolded petals
like a Venus upright in her seashell;
and the blushing one that, as if confused,
turns towards one that is more cool,
and how the cool one unfeelingly withdraws,
and how the cold one stands, wrapped in itself
among those open ones that shed everything.
And what they shed, how it can be light
and heavy, a cloak, a burden, a flight—
wing, a mask, or almost anything else,
and how they shed it: as if before the Beloved.

~

6/28 L'Isle sur la Sorgue

After leaving Aix, I make my way toward the haunts of another artist who, in a very different way from Cézanne, figures as a "source" of Rilke's poetry. I would like to explore the Vaucluse ("crossroads of Southern Europe") most particularly, to visit Carpentras and climb Mount Ventoux. But as my journey draws toward its close, time cuts ever more deeply into the grain of my imagination, and I have to settle for a side trip to the single spot most essential to the Petrarchan spirit; most crucial, at any rate, to the *Rime Sparse,* the poet's legacy of love.

As I sit inside the bus heading north, Provence passes by all too quickly outside. I pledge to myself that someday I will return and travel at a tempo more suitable to the aimless spirit of the wanderer. And yet, the express train through history that I am now on does have its own peculiar advantages. The pace makes a kind of compression chamber of my mind and eyes; requires a sort of concentration that is not necessarily unaesthetic. For the poet, too, must compress the wisdom of ages into a temporal vessel and try to contain timeless essences in fragile bottles of wine.

I cannot go all the way to Vaucluse today, but stop for the night at the little village of L'Isle sur la Sorgue. The name of place is indeed appropriate, for diverse branches of the river Sorgue cut right through the town, which (especially at night) looks like a miniature Venice, with its own small system of bridges, canals, and restaurants on the river. Yet L'Isle even has something that Venice does not, and I am fascinated by the huge waterwheels that churn rhythmically in the river, the moss-covered slats dripping silver necklaces as they turn around and around.

Leaning on a bridge, the stars above, and water reflecting light below, I while away the evening listening to the song of the Sorgue. Later that night, in a tiny room with a window open to the world, I float off to sleep and dream of a unique employment opportunity: an opening for a poet in *"Isle de la Cité,"* whose task it is to reinvent the wheel.

～

6/29 Fontaine-de-Vaucluse

Fontaine-de-Vaucluse— "Fountain of the Close Valley." As I take the winding path up the Sorgue early in the morning, the latter half of the name, at least, becomes transparent, for this "valley" is a veritable canyon. Rocky buttresses wall the water in on either side; here and there a line of trees, like daring climbers, scales the cliffs. On one of the rocky bluffs, one spies the remains of a 14th-century fortress, a red heraldic flag flying from the turret. But there is no question of any sort of cover on the face of the cliff that heads the canyon: the massive, sheer rise strikes me like the shaved face of a towering mountain. At its foot is the famous Fontaine, the spring that is the source of the Sorgue.

But I am not yet there, and here—a quarter-mile or so downstream—the Sorgue shoots by like a silver-blue bullet, as if it, too, were intent on ignoring the little businesses that have sprung up on its verdant banks. But there is one concern neither I, nor the river, can pass by without notice, because the *Moulin de papier* draws directly upon the power of the river: the medieval-style wooden hammers that pound the paper are driven by a glorious waterwheel exactly like those I saw at Isle. I promise myself that later I will stop in and examine the prize merchandise of the mill: poems that are printed on the paper produced there. Surely, I think, such sonnets must come from a distinguished stock.

For now, however, I merely pause to contemplate the water above the mill. There are few boulders here, and the river is deep and fast. Its color is astonishing: Though it can hardly possess the unfathomable depth of the Mediterranean, I am not sure I have ever seen such perfect *clarity* in the element. Gazing into this magic mirror, one can almost believe one is looking upon the archetype, the very *idea* of stained glass. And the color combination is ineffable: as if the water were simultaneously blue, green, and silver; as if the hues were matched yet unmixed; in love, and yet forever themselves.

Finally, I tear myself away from the reflection and proceed upstream toward the fount but almost immediately am confronted by a stone tablet set right into a rocky wall:

DANS CETTE VALLÉE CLOSE
EYVANT LES PLAISIRS DU SIÉCLE
Francois Pétrarque
VINT ABRITER SA MÉDITATION
EN L'AUTOMNE DE L'ANNÉE 1337
FIDÉLE AU CULTE DE **Laure**
ETA L'ÉTUDE DE L'ANTIQUÉ
NUl LIEU NE FUT PLUS CHER Á SON COEUR
NI PLUS PROPICE Á SA GLOIRE

LA VILLE DE VAUCLUSE Á SON POETE
AOÛT 1937

(In this close valley, to the delight of the ages, Francois Petrarch came to find refuge for his meditations in autumn of the year 1337, faithful to his worship of Laura, and his studies of Antiquity. No place was more dear to his heart, or more favorable to his fame.

—The town of Vaucluse to its Poet, August 1937)

The Sorgue near Fontaine-de-Vaucluse

At last, I measure the final steps to the fount. The cliff looms ahead, and the river grows markedly wilder, shooting through huge strewn boulders like rolling thunder. Here, the rushing Sorgue almost puts me in the mind of another fount of great poetry, the Vale of Chamouni; and yet nowhere does it really approach the savage sublimity of the dark Ravine of Arve. Even amidst the immensities of river, rock, and sky that stretch the limits of the imagination, the passionate enthusiasms of Nature maintain a certain decorum, an almost classical sense of proportion. If one climbs to the little observation hut up one steep, tree-lined wall, and so gains a bit of perspective on the roaring water, the scene will look less like a Rosa than a landscape by Poussin.

And then, finally, rising out from the base of the cliff: the fount itself, the mysterious source of the Sorgue.

No one no knows where, exactly, the Sorgue comes from. That is its mystery. There is no glacier melt feeding the river; no readily apparent origin for the river that flows forth from this fathomless fountain. And the adjective here is no mere poetic metaphor, but a matter of historical fact. Jacques Cousteau, legendary explorer of the deep blue sea, dived into the 400-meter deep pool to try to locate the source of the spring below the cliffs. Yet the secret remained safe even from Cousteau: In fact, this most skilled of divers almost lost his life in the ill-advised effort to plumb nature's hidden secret; underwater grottoes swallowed him, and he was lucky to make it out before his air supply ran out. No one since has attempted to use science to get to the bottom of this perpetual spring. The one thing we do know is that the *primary* source of the Sorgue is the rain that falls and runs down the face of the Vaucluse cliffs, and collects in grottoes underground. From there, it feeds the Fountain, this perpetual spring.

I myself am no scientist, and am not interested in tracing spiritual mysteries to their literal sources; I could have told Cousteau the attempt to reveal the secret of the Sorgue was a vain endeavor. What draws me is the spirit of the place, the symbolic meaning it contains, the message coded in the confluence of cliff, sky, and river; the way these "purely physical" elements combine to give birth to a new, palpably spiritual world:

FONTAINE-DE-VAUCLUSE

Soft rain falls
on the face
of the
cliff—

gathers

in dark
grottoes underground,
inside the looming rock before

bursting
forth from the source, the
Fountain of this
Close Valley
embracing
eternal spring—

and so am I
born
and
baptised
in Vaucluse

and poetry is the
aqueduct
of this

holy water, the

spirit

of

love . . .

Fontaine-de-Vaucluse

As I look into the Fontaine-de-Vaucluse, I see my reflection, and yet I barely recognize the face in the mirror, so changed is it from the one I once knew. In the first bloom of manhood, these features wore a cast of steady resolve as if united in purpose and sure of their ends. Then, these lips were flushed with red; and when they moved, I heard a voice I could call my own. Now they are wan and pale in the blue water, and tremble uncertainly in the waves. The motion of speech is upon them, and yet I hear no words, nor can I understand the sign language of this strange image, this second self that tries to communicate to me the mysteries of the Fount, the secret of the double life, the language of love.

Walking back from the Fount, I stop at the *Moulin de papier*. The waterwheel is turning round, powering large wooden mallets that pound pulp for paper. Flowers and leaves are put into the water that dyes the pulp, and so the finished sheets are littered with them. When the dark typeface is printed, the effect is that of a neat bouquet: small black roses amidst a bunch of light blue forget-me-nots and green herbs. But my mood is no longer full of spring, and I choose a paper with only a few red-brown leaves round the edges.

Later that afternoon, in a fit of youthful passion, I take another path, and keep going, climbing high, high up the side of the cliff above the fount itself. First, the domain of the fish, now the eagle—but, high as I go, I cannot climb or fly away from feelings at work within me. Walking amidst the woods and cliffs, far away from the crowds around the Sorgue, I recite my chosen poem; words I know by heart:

> *Alone and thoughtful, through deserted field*
> *I go with lowered head and measured pace,*
> *my eyes intent that I might flee in haste*
> *should any human footprint be revealed.*
> *I find no other shelter to conceal*
> *my burning heart than some secluded place,*
> *for once among the crowd my wretched face*
> *betrays the very flames it hoped to shield;*
> *so that by now I think the hills and stones,*
> *the rivers and the forests are aware*
> *of the life I lead, to others dim;*
> *and yet I find no path so overgrown*
> *that Love does not come with me everywhere,*
> *speaking with me the while, and I with him.*
> —Petrarch, *Canzoniere XXXV*

The night is restless and full of dreams.

6/30 Fontaine-de-Vaucluse (continued)

I am hardly the first American artist to have been impressed by the beauty of Vaucluse. Let us pretend that it is fall in the year 1841 (five years after the publication of Emerson's *Nature*) and that we are a famous American landscape artist, traveling abroad. Yesterday we boated down the Rhone from Lyon to Avignon; today, we've come here to admire—and paint—the magic of Vaucluse:

Oct 30, 1941 . . . At the upper end of the valley, from whence the water seemed first to burst forth, stood stupendous precipices, walls of perpendicular or impending rock scarred, scooped, marked, and stained, mounting to the sky—a strange and impressive scene! A few fruit-trees and small gardens fringed the water's edge; all else naked rocks, except here and there a few spots of sombre green, where some hardy plant found a crevice for its roots. The scene recalled to my mind my own picture of Infancy *in the* Voyage of Life, *where the stream issues from the foot of the mountain.*

. . . I then pursued my way towards the head of the vale: the grandeur of the scene increased at every step . . . A little higher still, and how the scene was changed! At the base of a precipice of vast height, was a basin of green water, deep and clear, of small extent, and exhibiting a surface but little troubled. I have seldom felt the sublimity of nature more deeply. There was no arch, no vault, and yet here came forth a river from the mysterious bosom of the earth, as gently as though it had been sleeping in its darkness.

—Thomas Cole, Correspondence

Cole arrived in stormy October, but today is the last of gentle June. As I take an early morning stroll up the Sorgue, the sun is breaking in this verdant close valley, trees and shrubs of all sorts bloom along the banks, and the looming cliffs seem a distant background to the almost pastoral setting. Yet, despite the generic change of season, our first impressions of Vaucluse did share a salient perspective. The Fontaine-de-Vaucluse furnished both of us with visions of our divine childhood; called to memory the nativity scenes in our own "Voyage of

Life." Why should the myth of the new world not be reborn in the baptismal font of the old?

∿

On the banks of the river, one-half mile downstream from the font, just above the bridge at the heart of the little village that takes its name from the Fontaine-de-Vaucluse, there is a congenial house with a beautiful courtyard and rose garden. This is Musée Pétrarque:

> Founded in 1927, under the aegis of the University of Aix-Marseille, it is heir to the Petrarquist tradition and to the taste for Italian studies which came back into vogue due to the Romantic aesthetic. Its installation in a 19th century house, on the left bank of the Sorgue, corresponds to the actual location of the poet's former residence.
>
> The museum includes the iconography supplied by drawings and prints of Petrarch, Laura, Avignon and Fontaine-de-Vaucluse as well as an estate of ancient editions of Petrarch's work, and those of French and Italian Petrarchists—a specialized library. The museographic purpose of the exhibitions is the birth and scope of the literary myth in restoring the character of the inspired spot that was Fontaine-de-Vaucluse. The presentation of the collections expresses the deep nature of Petrarchism: human experience as an allegory of love, and the spirituality of early humanism.

Wandering through the museum, I see more pictures of the Fontaine-de-Vaucluse, each with its own distinct perspective on the nature of the place; several of Petrarch's own most treasured books; images of the poet and his beloved Laura. Naturally, none of the latter are drawn from life, for while Nature is always willing to sit for a portrait, the spring of love is a secret affair, as deeply hidden as the source of the mysterious Fount itself. Though these fanciful likenesses are harmless enough, any attempt to frame the actual Laura was an endeavor every bit as vain as Cousteau's mechanical plumbing of the Fount; but this does not mean we have been left without any likeness of the poet's beloved. It is Petrarch's words themselves that are her true pictures, the dark veil that conceals the divine face even as it lets them be known.

And who could deny the sacredness of Love? Petrarch himself; the Christian philosopher who later moralized in Latin had many disparaging things to say about the Italianate passion that found expression in the immortal *Canzoniere*. But was this disparagement itself not just one more layer of protective covering, another kind of passionate disguise; one more character amongst the many that, in perpetual conversation with each other, compose the profile of his literary life?

Even so, as I wander through the museum, I must ask myself: Is the ethics enacted in the *Canzoniere* really compatible with theistic morality? Do the love poems complement or contest the privileging of the imperial papacy, the *myth of Rome* that plays so central a part in Petrarch's cultural vision? Malte, remember, gave expression to views on this subject that would be quite anathema to the poet crowned in the capital. I have to laugh silently to myself as I picture Petrarch in conversation with a character who could say:

> It did not astonish him that in this game there were
> several popes; he set Rome up yonder at the edge of the
> table, and here, under his right hand, was Avignon. He
> had no interest in Rome; for some reason or other he
> pictured it to himself as round, and dropped the matter
> there. But Avignon he knew . . . .

What a quaint and efficient disposal of the imperial city!

No matter; the initiator of Renaissance humanism's literary practice—especially the lyric tradition he inaugurated—opens onto horizons that stretch far beyond his peculiar culture-myth, or the religion ostensibly seated at its center. If it were not so, the Petrarchan leg of my voyage could be but a digressive aside, and I would be very surprised to stumble across traces of another poet's "ancestry" in this house; signs that confirm that I have in no wise strayed from my pilgrim-path in coming to Vaucluse. Amongst the very few books on sale at the front desk at Musée Pétrarque (all volumes indebted, one way or another, to the Poet of the Fount) I find a volume of poetry by Gaspara Stampa, the great (woman) lover remembered in the first of the *Duino Elegies*. Rilke's lines are well enough known; not so Gaspara Stampa's own.

On every Christmas her first love returns to her mind

> *I never see return that blessed day,*
> *When He was born, Himself the God of all,*
> *And took on flesh that He might wipe away*
> *Our father's sin against his maker's will,*
>
> *Without remembering the subtle skill*
> *With which Love caught me, spreading out his net*
> *Between the eyes and smile that haunt me still,*
> *Eyes far away that I cannot forget;*
>
> *And I cannot help but feel the ancient wound*
> *Which Love gave to my heart and my desires,*
> *So deep that wound was, and so harsh its pain;*
> *Did reason not take up its arms again*
> *To vanquish my senses, these consuming fires*
> *Would be such that no succor could be found.*

These lines are especially moving to me, for, like the speaker of this poem, I cannot see a nativity scene without remembering the designs of Love upon my own life. As I stroll in the Garden of the Musée Pétrarque, musing on that occasion when I was first touched by love's shaft, I think, too, of the lines I have composed in service to the god. They are undoubtedly Petrarchan, and yet I have this fearful confession to make: Though a poetic initiate of sorts, I cut a poor figure in life and cannot truly say that I have remained perfectly faithful to my Laura. I would have been, to be sure, but she who would be the object of my praise has changed face so many times since our first meeting that I think I should have to sketch the features of innumerable women to recall the one pure source of all my joy and sorrow.

And even if I should succeed in that; even if I should paint untold women in incomparable color, would not the portrait still be lacking and much left out of love's designs? For the mirror man finds in the face of woman is not like that of the *Fontaine*. The *speculum naturae* is, in some wise, constant: Winter may come, and cake the well with ice; the unruffled surface may be marred by stone from a careless hand; yet still, the spring keeps the secret of reflection safe inside and will soon, once again, return a faithful double to the searching eye. Not so the mirror of the mortal woman; once cracked, it is always broken and can never again return the image, the amulet, lost in the scattered shards.

But what true lover will let me speak such words without reproof? And I myself am ashamed to have spoken so poorly of the face that, if the truth be known, is really a perfect minia-ture of Nature, the only key to her diverse treasures. For the poet and lover, what is Earth but a box of misprized jewels; what history but Love's lost . . . and found?

In Memoriam FRANCESCO PETRARCA

Fontaine-de-Vaucluse

6/31/94

In the corner of what vast canvas
did Love first frame that face I know
altering the arm of Atlas
and bending light into a bow?

What sun god has ever striven
to recollect the rhyming rays
scattered when Love's car was driven
down history's back alley-ways?

Poet of the Fount! Your Lady's lines
are here remembered; sourceless eye
of our Love's aged wines

windowing the reason why
we were put upon this Earth
witnessing death, bearing

eternal birth.

I spend the rest of this, my last day chasing poetic shadows in the woods and garden paths, fishing for images in the Fount, and playing my small silver flute by the Sorgue. That night, I remember the dream I had in L'Isle, and the singular symbol of poetic vocation it contained. I did not know I would find another waterwheel here, in the natural palace that is Fontaine-de-Vaucluse; here, in the place that best favored Petrarch's poetic habit. With the silver waters of the Sorgue flowing through my mind, I take out a sketchpad and try my hand at my own paper mill; try to share with you, my friend, a little of what we've lost, and found:

Waterwheel

Two Sonnets *"sur Sorgue"*

SP II/26

> Stepsister of the Sorgue! Medieval moss-
> covered Moulin! Rain catered to compose
> the valley's verse: wood cross
> bound round to recreate the close
>
> of stone. Behind: the lean cliff lifts
> up from the cavernous crypts that carry
> spring inside: the silver song that sifts
> through revolutionary works that marry
>
> Man and Nature, Love and Labor, Words
> and World. Here are the small steps that turn
> rain into the sky where blackbirds
>
> fly: heaven in earth. The waterwheel
> sings to herself: ask the churn
> why she learns, and you hold Achilles' heel.

SP II/27

> Time-twirler! Well-tempered translator
> of flow into form—O lover of labor!
> The crest at the close—now, the strength of the satyr
> turns inside you into drumtap and tabor.
>
> World: will it stop for a second to see
> silver make paper? Above all—
> wasn't it sun, wasn't it summer that we re-
> printed before our long fall?

It bears, too—conceives—this cross of wood
and water. Is not the fruit fresh, this round tower
worth more than the press of the mass-produced hour?

Recurrent image: the fathomless grace
bound round the rim of the tempest-torn rood
splinters in circles, streamlining space.

Tonight, my last in this place of grace, and (*je regrette*) my last in France, I dine beneath the stars, on the banks of the Sorgue. The travelers at the hotel would have said that I was dining solo; you, on the other hand, have been with me for some time now, and perhaps would like to join me for this last supper?

SP II/19

God's mouth is full of holes. When heaven
smiles, stars fall out and every thing
starts over: this fruit and this fish are the leaven
of love. When we clasp hands and sing

we silver like a serving dish, bearing the strange
being-enframed which, in time, makes us
human. Just think of the rainbow-bending range
of colors caught in the clear, confused fuss

of flowers that press our face. A soul's poem—
how could it ever end? How could a woman
ever reseal why? The fisherman

dreams deadpan. So let's just say home
is here, now—in the long song-line I give
to you; this gold scale in this silver sieve.

≈

The Rhone near Raron

4

Crossroads

Swiss Valais:
Sierre/Raron

7/1 en route to the Swiss Valais

I am up early for the trip to my final destination: the Swiss Valais.
As I cross the border into Switzerland, leaving France behind, a
tear falls from my eye, for I think it has been a memorable visit,
and I feel as if I am leaving a newfound love. But I will return,
will I not?

As the train rumbles on, the landscape changes. My
entrance into Switzerland is graced by the alpine beauty of
Lake Geneva, the silver surface like an interior sea beneath
the rocky rise of mountains. Yet for me, this great lake is but
a temporary widening of the river that binds the post-Parisian
chapter of my trip together; the Rhone runs through the Swiss
Valais before making its way down toward Provence and into
the Mediterranean. The poetic significance of this fact was
not lost on Rilke, who—traveling "downstream"—penned this
letter from Geneva after a stay in Valais:

> How beautiful this Valais really is. The impressions of
> Sion and Sierre have at one stroke made my Swiss recollec-
> tions, already so various, more complete by much, as always
> happens whenever I get to the Rhone—: its banks smile at me
> with a wonderful friendliness—as though this stream more
> than any other had the power to make its own the lands that
> it refreshes: Vaucluse, Avignon, the Ile de Bartelasse and this
> uncanny Jonction here: all of them are related by marriage and
> akin through the spirit of this river—and now at last, in the
> generous valleys of the Valais, what room it has to spread out
> and be itself in every curve . . . the Valais is a plain a long way
> from the mountains; and these are themselves no more than a
> background, conveying no effect of weight and with slopes so
> hazy that at times they seem imaginary, like the mountains
> pictured in a reflection . . . .

A little more than a year later, Rilke was once more in the region and once more dwelling on the spirit of the Rhone:

To Princess Marie von Thurn und Taxis-Hohenlohe

Hotel Chateau Bellevue
Sierre (Valais)
July 25, 1921

It is getting toward the end of July, and I am not with you. Don't prepare any room for me yet, but also don't pronounce the death sentence yet on my coming: in August perhaps.

In these last weeks I have often come very near announcing my visit, and a peculiar current came into my rather sluggish spirit whenever I wanted to do so; but what holds me on the other hand is this wonderful Valais: I was imprudent enough to travel down here, to Sierre and Sion; I have told you what a singular charm these regions exercised over me when I first saw them last year at the time of the vintage: the circumstance that in the physiognomy of the landscape here Spain and Provence so strangely interact struck me immediately even then: for both landscapes spoke to me in the last years before the war more strongly and decisively than anything else; and now to find their voices united in an outspread mountain valley of Switzerland! And this echo, this family likeness is no imagination. Just recently I read in a brief treatise on the plant life of the Wallis that certain flowers appear here which are otherwise found only in Provence and Spain; it is the same with the butterflies: thus does the spirit of a great river (and to me the Rhone has always been one of the most wonderful) bear endowments and kinships through the countries. Its valley here is so wide and so grandly filled out with little heights within the frame of the big border mountains that the eye is continually provided with a play of the most delightful changes, a chess game with hills, as it were. As if even hills were still being shifted and distributed—so like Creation in its effect is the rhythm in the arrangement, with every

point of view astonishingly new, of what one beholds—, and
the old houses and castles move the more delightfully in these
optical games since for the most part they again have the slope
of a vineyard, the wood, the woodland meadow or the gray rock
as background, as incorporate in it as pictures in a tapestry; for
the most indescribable (almost rainless) sky takes part from far
above in these perspectives and animates them with so spiritual
an atmosphere that the special way things stand to each other
seems, quite as in Spain, to exhibit at certain hours that tension
which we think to perceive between the stars of a constellation.

So it is this Valais, where Rilke spent most of the last years
of his life and finally accomplished his poetic mission; this
Valais, where he lies beneath a gravestone bearing an epitaph of
his own composing; that will be the final stop of my old world
journey, the Mecca of my pilgrim path.

By the time I arrive in Sierre, it is evening. The still slightly
silver Rhone runs through the town; mountains, vague in
evening's twilight, rise like an enormous rampart around it. And
Sierre seems to mark an invisible linguistic boundary. Here, for
the first time, I am not really a tongue-tied foreigner, but hear
and speak the poet's primary language for the first time.

~

7/2   Sierre/ Raron

I have but a single day to spend in the Swiss Valais. Up early, I
am on my way through the vineyards above Sierre to the locus
of much of Rilke's most inspired poetry: the Château de Muzot.
Rilke's letter continues with details of his discovery of Muzot;

. . . But now to the particulars of my being detained: when
I departed from Etoy about three weeks ago (with my visitor),
we were offered the prospect (we did not want to stay long in

the hotel) of a little house here which on sight proved imprac-
tical; we looked at some others in the neighborhood, the time
passed—until suddenly an object of the greatest temptation
appeared. This old manoir; a tower, whose walls go back to the
thirteenth century, whose beamed ceilings and furnishings too
in part (chests, tables, chairs) date from the seventeenth,—was
for sale or for rent. At a very cheap price, but still far beyond the
possibilities I could realize in Swiss Francs. Then last week one
of my friends, who had known this so-called Château de Muzot
(pronounced Muzotte) for a long time, one of the Reinharts of
Winterthur meted the house in order to place it at my disposal!
And now I am moving out there tomorrow and will make a little
attempt at dwelling in these rather stern castle circumstances
that cleave to one like a suit of armor! I really had to do that,
didn't I?

So began Rilke's stay at Muzot, one that—in February
1922—finally saw him attain the object of his lifelong poetic
quest: the realization of the *Duino Elegies,* begun almost 10
years before in Princess Marie's castle near Duino, Italy. And
in the same miraculous days of inspiration, another, unantic-
ipated work was born—the joyful complement to the *Elegies'*
lamentations; Rilke's *Sonnets to Orpheus.*

My own visit to the site is beset with uncertainty; before my
arrival here, I had no idea whether or not Château de Muzot
still existed. I had written the Sierre tourist bureau inquiring
about it well in advance of my departure, enclosing Rilke's
description of the site for reference:

[Muzot] lies about twenty minutes quite steep above Sierre,
in a less arid, happy rusticity with many springs tumbling
through it,—with views into the valley, over to the mountain
slopes and into most wonderful depths of sky. A little rustic
church, situated above somewhat to the left in the vineyards
(no longer visible in the picture), belongs to it. The picture does

not do Muzot justice, the tree growth in the garden has become much taller in the meantime, also one does not see the magnificent old poplar which should be imagined a few steps farther forward, to the right beyond the edge of the picture, and which is characteristic of the aspect of the little castle from wherever one sees it. I myself say "little castle", for this is the perfect type of the medieval manoir as it still survives everywhere here . . . .

If the Swiss were as punctual as their watches, I would have had information about the present status of Muzot before I left for France; but, as it was, I found out only yesterday that—yes—Château de Muzot was very much in existence; was, in fact, privately owned and lived in. I could not, therefore, enter Muzot; however, it was possible to view it from the outside. This prospect was quite enough to excite my anticipation: even an exterior view of the Château de Muzot would, I felt, open a window onto the Rilke's world.

. . . On the (second) story I have established myself. There is my little bedroom which receives its light through the windowpane at the right, but also on the other side sends out a little balcony into the tree. The double window beside it and around the corner, the next window in the sunlit west front belong to my workroom, which we just about finished fitting out yesterday, all with appurtenances at hand: it has all kinds of promise and attraction for me, with its old chests, its oak table of 1600 and the old dark beam ceiling into which is carved the date MDCXVII; when I say attraction, that is nevertheless not accurate: for actually all of Muzot, while it somehow holds me, yet also drives a kind of worry and oppression into my spirit; as far as possible, I have familiarized myself with its oldest history . . .

As I set off on foot for Muzot, local map in hand, the city of Sierre itself seems to direct me towards my goal. As I walk up a little street several blocks from my hotel, I observe a large house with a particularly attractive iron grille gateway and solid steps leading to an elaborate arched door. On the second floor, directly above the doorway, there is a small balcony, the shuttered entrance to which is half-open, as if someone had just gone inside. This is almost the sole building on the street; nonetheless, it is a little surprising to see the address—a bold and singular number "1" displayed next to the door. And then I notice the name on the corner of the street; all this time, I have, without deliberate intent, been walking *"Rue Rainer Maria Rilke"!*

Rue Rilke

After a moment of silence, I continue on the path to Rilke's Muzot.

> *. . . the de Blonays probably built it; in the fifteenth century it was in the possession of the de la Tournay-Chastillons; at the beginning of the sixteenth, a year before the battle of Marignan, the wedding of Isabelle de Chevron and Jean de Montheys took place there (all the guests of those three days of continuous*

festivity are still known and who walked with whom—). Jean de Montheys fell at Marignan and was brought back to the young widow at Muzot. Immediately thereafter the passions of two suitors became kindled for her, who in their fire fell out so violently that they ran each other through in a duel. The unhappy Isabelle, who seemed to have borne the loss of her husband with dignity, did not get over this annihilation of both her wooers, between whom she herself had not yet chosen; she lost her reason and thereafter left Muzot only by night, giving the slip to the solicitude of her old nurse Ursule; almost every night one could see her, "tres legerement habillee", wandering to Miege to the grave of her two hot-blooded suitors, and the legend goes that finally on a winter's night she was discovered stiff and dead in the graveyard at Miege.—So for this Isabelle or for the dead Montheys returning over and over, like a pendulum, from Marignan, one must somehow prepare oneself and may be astonished at nothing.

Once I leave the center of Sierre, the roads grows steep, curving ever more ambitiously up the slope behind the town. Though the density of the houses naturally thins dramatically, the hillside above Sierre is never truly wild; the scene is, no doubt, very much altered since the time Rilke lived here 70 years ago. What I am walking through now looks like a well-off suburb and is not particularly unusual, except that I am walking at a 45-degree angle and that many of these plots boast several acres of vineyards in their backyards. But Muzot, I expect, will be something else.

The Château de Muzot, now that we have cleaned it out, has gained everywhere in brightness and homeliness. The rooms, as in all these medieval houses, have about them something honest— farmerish, rude, without arriere-pensees ... Nevertheless—, and so that I don't forget it, beside my bedroom, in the upper story, the so-called old "chapel" lies out behind, a little white-washed room, accessible from the hallway through a surprisingly low, still quite medieval gothic doorway, and above it in the wall, as a relief standing sharply out, not, as you might think, the cross, but: a big swastika!

As I approach the place where I believe Muzot should be, the land unclutters. There is more vineyard, more earth, less driveway. If I leapfrogged these foothills, I would be in the lap of a mountain: On either side of the valley, impressive peaks rise toward the sky. Yet, as Rilke said, they remain, somehow, distant—and besides, right now, I am not interested in mountains, but in the island of trees I see just ahead, and the lonely dwelling I think I see nestled amongst gardens and vineyards. If I am not mistaken, I am approaching Château de Muzot.

Château de Muzot

So you see me then, Princess, for the immediate future under the spell of this Muzot: I must try it. If you could see it! When one approaches from the valley, it stands there every time like an enchantment above the now already scorched rose paths of its little garden, in its color of ancient hew stone that has gray and violet tones, but has roasted and browned itself golden in the sun, again like certain walls in Andalusia . . .

Muzot, indeed. The quaint yet stern countenance of the building nicely counterpoints the lacy trees that brush its stoic masonry. There is the small balcony cut into the stone; on the far side of the low garden wall, a tasteful flower garden flourishes in the courtyard; and—perhaps, most importantly: *"the magnificent poplar which should be imagined . . . beyond the edge of the picture . . ."*

SO I/1

A tree ascended. O pure transcendence!
Orpheus is singing! O tall tree in the ear!
And everything hushed. Yet in that quiet cadence
new transformations were beginning to appear.

Creatures of calm thronged out of the trans-
parent wood, out from their nest and lair,
and it so happened that it was neither fear
nor cunning that led their silent dance

but hearing. Growl and roar, shriek and hiss
seemed small inside their hearts. And where
there was barely a hut to receive all this—

a covert composed of darkest love and fearing
where trembling fence-posts marked a clearing,
you built them temples in the open ear.

It is not difficult to imagine Rilke dwelling here, wandering amidst the roses and then retreating into his "suit of armor" to write the letters and poems that flowed like water from his pen. And yet, it is rather difficult to sense the *Elegies* in this landscape. This is not terribly surprising, for Muzot was not the origin of this cathedral of verse—Rilke's Chartres, or Notre Dame. The *Duino Elegies* are (according to Rilke's own inscription) "The Property of Princess Marie von Thurn und Taxis Hohenlohe"; they "belong" to the much larger and more rugged castle owned by the Princess—the castle of Duino—where they were first conceived in 1912. The story of their inception is well known: Rilke pacing on the bastions overlooking the raging sea like some Hamlet before the storm; and then, the angelic voice speaking to him, delivering the opening lines of the *Elegies*:

Who if I cried, would hear me amongst the angelic
orders? And even if one of them pressed me suddenly
against his heart, I would be consumed
in his stronger existence . . .

Yet it was not Rilke's lot to complete this poem, which he regarded as the fulfillment of his poetic destiny, in one fell swoop; on the contrary, there was a long and tortuous path between conception and delivery. Rilke did complete a draft of the First Elegy on that stormy day in January 1912; shortly afterwards, the Second Elegy was largely accomplished; and portions of several of the others were written in various places in subsequent years. The Third—begun at Duino—was finished in Paris in 1913; the Fourth in Munich in November of 1915. This Fourth Elegy, in particular, bespeaks the bitterness of a soul, and world, at war.

In Rilke's own mind, it was, indeed, the cataclysm of the First World War that obstructed the path of the *Elegies,* that laid waste the inner resources he required for their completion.

For many years, Rilke—though he had always had a definite idea of the design of the whole—could make no progress on his masterwork. At times, he feared the work would be aborted. War-torn Germany, in particular, seemed an inhospitable place to accomplish his aims. In 1919, Rilke departed Germany (he had been living in Munich) for Switzerland with the hope of finding a spiritual refuge, one that would allow him to reconnect with the angelic inspiration that had spoken to him at Duino seven years earlier. In August of 1921, a friend's generosity made it possible for him to domicile himself here, at Muzot.

And the poet did, indeed, finally accomplish his mission in his "little castle," though only *after* an unexpected turn in his literary life. The flow of inspiration that finally consummated Rilke's poetic career did not resume with work on the *Elegies* themselves, but rather with an entirely new opus that owed its inspiration to less angelic sources:

SO I/2

> *And it was a girl, almost, who emerged from*
> *the consonant pleasure of song and lyre*
> *and shone clear through her shady spring attire*
> *and made her bed within my ear's deep drum.*
>
> *And slept in me. And her sleep was everything.*
> *The meadows that held eternal wonder, these*
> *palpable horizons, the immeasurable trees*
> *and each stone set in my self's ring.*
>
> *She slept the world. Singing God, how*
> *did you perfect her, so she never yearned*
> *to be awake? See, she arose, and slumbered.*
>
> *Where is her death? O, find the theme now*
> *before the bright candle of your song is burned.*
> *Where is she descending? ... A girl, almost, numbered ...*

The story of the genesis of Rilke's *Sonnets to Orpheus*—
though less supernaturally charged than the angelic shout that
opened the *Elegies*—is no less significant to the understanding
of the processes of his poetic creation. Years before his stay at
Muzot, Rilke and his wife, Clara, had been friends with the
parents of a young girl with a natural talent and love for dance.
The girl's mother later wrote him that while her daughter was
still a child "the art of movement and metamorphosis innate
in her body and mind" was already remarkable. As the girl
approached puberty, however, she unexpectedly announced
that she could or would no longer dance; this was the first sign
of the mysterious glandular disease that was to determine her
fate. After resigning dance, the girl took up music, and then,
subsequently, drawing "as if the dancing which had been
denied were still manifesting itself in her, but more and more
gently and discreetly." All too soon, death claimed its own:
One year after the end of the war, the strange illness took the
life of Vera Ouckama Knoop at the age of 19.

Rilke learned of Vera's story while staying at Muzot and,
much moved by it, instinctively felt its underlying connection
with his own poetic calling. On New Year's Eve (1921/2) Rilke
wrote Frau Knoop:

*Were one to read this about any young girl one had
not known, it would touch one nearly enough. And now it
concerns Vera, whose dark, singularly composed charm is to
me so utterly unforgettable and so incredibly recall-able that at
the very moment of writing this I would fear to close my eyes
lest I suddenly feel myself, here, in my present consciousness,
completely overwhelmed by it.*

*How much, how very, very much she was all that, that to
which these recollections of your suffering bear such deep irrevocable witness,—and, isn't it so? How wonderful, how unique,
how incomparable a human being is! There now arose, when
everything was allowed to use itself up suddenly which otherwise*

*might have lasted for a long being—here (where?),—there now
arose this excess of light in the girl's heart, and in it appear so
infinitely illumined the two extreme borders of her pure insight:
this, that pain is a mistake, a mute misunderstanding, bodily
in origin, that drives its wedge, its stony wedge, into the unity
of heaven and earth—, and on the other side this harmonious
being—one of her heart, opened to everything, with this unity
of the existing and continuing world, this acceptance of life, this
joyful, this much-moved, this to ultimate capacity belonging way
into the here and now—alas, only into the here and now?! No,
(which she could not know in those first attacks of breakup and
farewell!)—into the whole, into a far more than here and now. Oh,
how, how she loved, how she reached with her heart's antennae
out beyond everything here graspable and embraceable—, in
those sweet hovering pauses in pain, that, full of the dream of
recovery, were still granted her . . . .*

SO I/25

*But you—so swiftly departed—you whom I
loved like a flower whose name I do not know,
you will I once more remember, and show—
lovely playmate of the unconquerable cry.*

*A dancer first, whose body's sudden pause
froze as if youth were cast in bronzed art
mourning and listening. Then, from higher laws
music fell into her transfigured heart.*

*Illness was near. Already caught by shadow
the pulsing blood darkened. Still, as if all might go
forward, it pressed on towards its natural spring.*

*Seized by dark stuttering, more and more
it gleamed of earth. Until—with horrible pounding—
it stepped through the desolate open door.*

The chief motifs of the *Sonnets* (love, death, transformation) resonate with those of the *Elegies;* it is thus not surprising
that the story of Vera—whose life and death is itself tragedy
transformed—should find expression in a work that would not
only complement the *Elegies* but catalyze their completion. But
still more interesting are the quite distinct points of departure
for Rilke's "diptych": on the one hand, the disembodied, angelic
voice speaking to him in the midst of a storm; on the other, the
death of an artistically gifted young girl.

But Vera's story in itself was not enough to inspire the
Sonnets; Rilke's muse required other preparation. Paul Valery's
L'âme et la danse, which he was reading at the time, also linked
the motifs of dance and metamorphosis, but another biographical source for the *Sonnets to Orpheus* will have still more
significance for us since we have come to Muzot fresh from the
Fontaine-de-Vaucluse.

Rilke often prepared for his own original poetic production by writing letters; he also primed his own imagination by
producing prose and verse translations. In January 1922, Rilke,
with the aid of a friend who supplied him with the original
text and a dictionary, prepared to complete a translation of
a Latin letter by Petrarch; work he had already begun some
years before in Paris. The project was never completed; a
biographical source informs us that Rilke's Petrarch translation
was *"abandoned"* on account of the flow of inspiration that, in
the first days of February, resulted in the 26 sonnets that (with
a few changes and additions) comprise the whole of the first
cycle of the work that truly "belongs" here, to this site, and the
memory of the graceful young Vera.

Our biographer is, no doubt, literally correct; I, however,
would prefer to consider the matter in a different light and
consider Rilke's intended "Petrarch translation" not so much
abandoned, as transformed, *metamorphosed* into a far more
original form.

And that is the beginning of the end of our—of Rilke's—
story. After the breakthrough represented by the first cycle
of sonnets, the poet's projected work completed itself with
miraculously efficiency. The *Elegies*—in painful gestation for
a decade—were completed in a matter of days; subsequently,
the second cycle of (29) sonnets came into being. By the 23rd
of February (approximately three weeks after the first sonnet
was written) the centerpiece of Rilke's poetic testament—the
Duino Elegies, and their more joyful counterpart, the *Sonnets
to Orpheus*—was complete. His poetic mission accomplished,
Rilke was, in his own eyes, redeemed.

Die Sonette an Orpheus	Duineser Elegien
geschrieben als ein Grabmal	aus den Besitz
für	der Fürstin
Vera Ouckama Knoop	Marie von Thurn und Taxis Hohenlohe
^^^^^^^^^^	^^^^^^^^

CHÂTEAU DE MUZOT
FEBRUARY
1922

~

"Will metamorphosis."
—Rilke

Retiring to a little creek that flows by Muzot, I open the volume
of the *Sonnets to Orpheus* I have brought with me here. It has
always seemed to me that these verses were sent to me, person-
ally—that these words were a letter posted to my address—but
then, perhaps that is not very surprising, because I tend to read
most poetry that way. Nonetheless, there is something special

about these verses, composed 70 years ago here, at Muzot; something that has already moved me to try to carry on the correspondence, as if the words were part of a chain that I did not wish to break. Perhaps this feeling is behind the destination of some of my own verses, the address of which is inevitably different from Rilke's own. If Rilke composed his Sonnets *to* Orpheus, it was only logical that I should send mine—not to Orpheus himself—but to the one to whom he addressed his song, his psyche or soul, his Eurydice.

SP I/19

> *Yet you will I now, you whom first I saw*
> *a flower whose kind I could not know*
> *yet once again remember and seek to show*
> *little lines that lilt in love with law.*
>
> *First a friend and then—nothing—but a face*
> *filled with stars; as if planets poured*
> *night into your eyes, and seasons scored*
> *cycles in the lift of that black lace.*
>
> *But day breaks dream, and the style*
> *of virgin glance cannot long beguile*
> *worlds that will the wither of the rose, unless—*
>
> *again and again, we daredevilishly confess*
> *the content of our care, so love shade grows*
> *glass gardens, and makes heaven of our prose.*

In the midst of poetic reflection, my mind wanders back to all the historic sights I have seen on this voyage, but none speak to me like the row of flowers here, in the garden at Muzot, the red emperors that remind me of my own poetic home and future estate.

SP II/5

> Fresh flower-mouth just now beginning
> to mime the drama of the dawn
> open, until the sense of such sweet sinning
> strews emperors across the lawn.
>
> Friend: the star form of your face—
> red petal of endless falls—
> holds the lost love of the race
> so even his house calls
>
> cannot brim the bright container
> or count the varied kinds
> of visionary color mixing in our minds.
>
> But he—impatient!—why can he never wait
> to lift that face to fate
> or see his story stain her?

Yet so soon as these words are out of my mouth, the timeworn grace of Muzot looms like a kind of admonition, reminding me that these historic walls were the enclosure for Rilke's inspiration and that they, and the characters of consciousness they signify, need to be *recontained* in the vision of verse. If the flowers spoke to me of a new beginning, that new age could only be born as another draft—a graft—of the poet's own, just as he himself had hybridized new and old worlds here in Muzot.

SP II/6

Emperor! Red dramaturge of days
ancient as the eyes of time
container of the waterways
that spill the world of rhyme

Your coffers hold casts of clothes
all kings and Calibans—
yet each petal is the molt of moths—
Icarian wing-span.

Star centuries send fresh perfume
recanonizing the class
of royalty rented by the room

so dustcovered crowns can dance
like fireflies in long dark grass
red rubies—meet—as if—by chance—

~

After Rilke completed the *Elegies* and *Sonnets* in February of
1922, Muzot remained his more or less permanent residence
until his death (due to illness) in 1926. He did not, moreover,
resign the pen after the completion of the *Elegies* and
Sonnets; his continuing literary output included, for instance,
numerous poems in French. However, the *Duino Elegies* and
Sonnets to Orpheus remain the great testament of the late
Rilke, and much of his most compelling subsequent work—
much of it in the form of correspondence composed here, at
Muzot—can readily be understood as (partial) interpretations
of the "philosophy" and "religion" embodied in the poetry.
The "letters from Muzot" thus comprise an important part
of this little castle's monumental legacy to humankind, and
we take leave of Rilke's "suit of a(r)mor" with passages from a

letter composed here; one that touches upon the heart of his vision of humankind.

To Countess Margo Sizzo

Chateau de Muzot sur Sierre,
Epiphany (January 6), 1923:

. . . . I do not like the Christian conceptions of a Beyond, I am getting farther and farther away from them, naturally without thought of attacking them; they may have their right and persistence beside so many other hypotheses about the periphery of the divine,—but to me they contain above all the danger not only of making those who have vanished more imprecise to us and above all more inaccessible—; but we too, drawing ourselves yonder in our longing and away from here, we ourselves become thereby less definite, less earthly: which for the present, so long as we are here and akin to tree, flower and soil, we do have, in a purest sense, to remain, even still to become!

As concerns myself, what has died for me has died, so to speak, into my own heart: the vanished person, when I have looked for him, has collected himself singularly and so surprisingly in me, and it was moving to feel that for us he was now only there, that my enthusiasm for serving his existence there, for deepening and glorifying it, took the upper hand almost at the very moment in which pain would otherwise have invaded and laid waste the entire landscape of my spirit . . .

. . . so deep is death implanted in the nature of love that (if only we are cognizant of it without allowing ourselves to be misled by the uglinesses and suspicions we attached to it) it nowhere contradicts love: whither after all can it drive someone we have born unutterably in our heart save into this very heart, where would the "idea" of this loved person be, indeed his ceaseless influence (for how could that cease which even

while he lived with us was more and more independent of his tangible presence) . . . where would this always secret influence be held more secure than in us? Where can we come closer to it, where more purely celebrate it, when obey it better, than when it appears linked with our own voices, as if our heart had learned a new language, a new song, a new strength.

I reproach all modern religions for having handed to their believers consolations and glossings over of death, instead of administering to them the means of reconciling themselves to it and coming to an understanding with it. With it, with its full unmasked cruelty: this cruelty is so tremendous that it is just with it that the circle closes: it leads right back again into the extreme of a mildness that is great, pure and perfectly clear (all consolation is turbid) as we have never surmised mildness to be, not even on the sweetest spring day. But towards the experiencing of this most profound mildness which, were only a few of us to feel it with conviction, could perhaps little by little penetrate and make transparent all the relations of life: toward the experiencing of this richest and soundest mildness, mankind has never taken even the first step—unless in its oldest, most innocent times, whose secret has been all but lost to us. The content of "initiations" was, I am sure, nothing but the imparting of a "key" that permitted the reading of the word "death" without negation; like the moon, life surely has a side permanently turned away from us which is not its counter-part but its complement toward perfection, toward consummation, toward the really sound and full sphere and orb of being.

One should not fear that our strength might not suffice to bear any experience of death, even were it the nearest and the most terrible; death is not beyond our strength; it is the measure mark at the vessel's rim: we are full as often as we reach it, and being full means (for us) being heavy . . . that is all. I will not say that one should love death; but one should love life so magnani-

mously, so without calculation and selection that spontaneously one constantly includes with it and loves death too (life's averted half), which is in fact what happens also, irresistibly and illimitably, in all great impulses of love! Only because we exclude death in a sudden moment of reflection, has it turned more and more into something alien, and as we have kept it in the alien, something hostile.

It is conceivable that it stands infinitely closer to us than our effort would allow—this has grown ever clearer to me with the years, and my work has perhaps only the one meaning and mission to bear witness, more and more impartially and independently . . . more prophetically perhaps, if that does not sound too arrogant . . . to this insight which so often unexpectedly overwhelms me . . . our effort I mean, can only go toward postulating the unity of life and death, so that it may gradually prove itself to us. Prejudiced as we are against death, we do not manage to release it from its misrepresentations . . . only believe, dear, dear Countess, that it is a friend, our deepest friend, perhaps the only one who is never, never, to be misled through our behavior and vacillation . . . and that, it is understood, not in the sentimental-romantic sense of denying life, of life's opposite, but our friend just when we most passionately, most vehemently assent . . . to being-here, to functioning, to Nature, to love. Life always says simultaneously Yes and No. Indeed, death (I adjure you to believe!) is the true yeasayer. It says only: Yes. Before eternity.

Think of the "Slumbering Tree." Yes, how good that it occurs to me. Think of all the little pictures and inscriptions to it—how, in youthful innocent trust, you there constantly recognized and affirmed both in the world: the sleeping and the waking, the bright and the dark, the voice and the silence . . . la présence et l'absence. All the apparent opposites which somewhere come together in one point, which at one place sing the hymn of their wedding—and this place is—for the time being—our heart!

~

Raron Church

Raron

. . . a small village east of Sierre; after a short train ride along the
Rhone, I arrive at the mountainous and rustic little town where
the poet is buried. The gravesite, I am told, lies atop the nearest
foothill, in a churchyard cemetery a few kilometers from the
train. I set off at a quick pace, but my progress is soon inter-
rupted by the river. Stopping on the long swinging footbridge,
I gaze upstream. From this vantage, the Rhone seems to pour
forth from the towering snow-covered mountains like wine
from heaven poured upon this good earth. This river has been
the lifeblood of my pilgrim way.

The poet's gravesite is a "local attraction." There are any number of signs posted in the city pointing the way to *Burgkirche/Grabstätte Rilke*. These in themselves are quite necessary; the way through the winding streets of this medieval-seeming Swiss town is by no means clear, and the path to the churchyard longer and steeper than one expects. But the various concerns that attempt to capitalize on the poet's name—such as one that sells Rainer Maria Rilke Wine—are less appreciated.

After winding through the town, I am finally making my way up the hillside to the church. The scenery is fine; small, attractive Swiss dwellings set into the hillside, often adorned by flourishing flowers. And now, the church—high on the hillside, commanding a view of the valley—is just ahead.

I enter the churchyard through an old rustic gate and am immediately dispossessed; assaulted by an army of rather gaudy gravestones, most of which sport ugly, literalistic depictions of Christ on the cross. I find the whole effect repugnant—as if it were necessary to mount a crusade on behalf of the dead, as if corpses went to church.

Raron Churchyard

My heart sinking, I look around. How am I going to find Rilke's gravestone? There are no directive signs here, and I can hardly imagine that the Poet is to be found in this disenchanted plot. But there are two visitors just on their way out, and I am relieved when they direct me to the far side of the church, where, I am assured, I will find what I am seeking.

And so I turn the corner and breathe a sigh of relief. I've come out to a small side yard that commands a gorgeous prospect of the Valais; there are mountains on all sides, the silver thread of the Rhone in the valley, and here—all by itself against the wall of the church, an ivy-covered stone. There is no cross, but this inscription:

RAINER MARIA RILKE

ROSE, OH REINER WIDERSPRUCH.
LUST,
NIEMANDES SCHLAF ZU SEIN
UNTER SOVIEL
LIDERN*

*Rose, oh pure contradiction/the desire/to be nobody's sleep/ under so many/lids

I see that those who have come before me are true pilgrims, too; on the green earth below the stone, there is a fresh red rose.

I cried grievously at Rilke's grave. I very much doubt that the sensations I felt were much different from those a lover might feel at the grave a lost beloved, for where it is love that binds souls, what does it matter, finally, whether the other with whom we share the mystery of being is friend or lover, man or woman, dead or alive? But my grief was tempered with the joy of communion, even victory, as if I too had arrived at some kind of goal: no *end*, certainly, but, perhaps, a new beginning. Neither Rilke nor Orpheus would have it any other way.

Rilke's grave

SO I/5

Erect no memorial. Only let the rose
bloom each year for his sake.
For Orpheus is. His metamorphoses
in this thing and that. We shouldn't take

pains over other names. Once and for all
it's Orpheus, when it sings. He comes and goes.
Isn't it already much if his dying notes fall,
sometimes, a short while after the rose?

O how he must vanish, so you might see!
Even if he feared that he might disappear.
When his words surpass all that's here

he's already There, beyond your company.
The lyre's lattice does not restrain his hands.
And he trespasses, as his heart commands.

~

Did you take me at my word? Or did you nonetheless believe the grave would mark "the end" of this story? I wish it could be so, but history does not allow us to rest in peace. I must tell you, now, about what so disturbed me on way to Rilke's grave.

In Raron

I have already hinted at it. The path to Rilke's grave was paved with crosses; the image of the crucified son apprehended one at every twist in the road, every turn of the trail. Though it was almost against my will, I had found I could not help documenting the phenomenon; here I was, a pilgrim desiring to pay homage to his master—to honor a bond, and confirm a carrying out of the work—and I could hardly see a single Tree of Life on account of the forest of crosses. Fountains, flower boxes, tree trunks; all sprouted one or another image of the crucified son.

I came to study life and death, but my vision was obstructed by the rabid repetition of this image, this visual hyperbole that dominated the field of vision. How long are we going to believe that the whole of the true work we have to do was ever or could ever be the magic spell of one man? It is not, for a moment, against the man Jesus that I speak; on the contrary, I speak rather in his behalf—on behalf, so to speak, of his salvation. I speak against the appearance of an obsessive, mindless, loveless, unbeautiful repetition of crosses—the cancer of the cross strewn across the landscape of the human imagination that is, literally, killing him, and us, all over again, all the time. The image of the crucifixion, of Jesus on the cross, is an empty sign, its meaning monstrously disfigured by now, and has been made to mean the reverse of the real revelation it contains, *for the cross has become . . . a defense against death!* And that means: a defense against facing the true meaning of life; including— *especially—Jesus' life;* a defense against *interpretation,* the act of carrying forward the work of his words and signs in the ongoing labor of love that is the life of the spirit. It is his ghost that calls upon me—upon us—to look, to learn, to love and to write—to break, and remake, the chains.

For it is not only the death penalty that is a caricature of Christ. Who can doubt that Jesus' image has become a form of

... self-caricature? We must work to release him from the hell of senseless adulation—for this, indeed, is the true hell; it is no infernal region where devils gnash their teeth and grin in the midst of fiery cauldrons, but that place in mind where the image repeats, again and again, without change, without movement, without transformation. Mental fixation forges the chains of hell and "religion"—as this has too often been understood— is a form of mental fixation. No wonder hymns of heaven so often result in hells on earth, and murderers of men and women lift up their voice in praise of "God."

But let us come, once more, to Orpheus. I had read one Orpheus poem at Rilke's grave; now, wandering farther up the path behind the church, feeling the spirit of beauty so present everywhere in nature, I sat on a rustic bench, to read the Orpheus poem—the last poem in the first part of Rilke's cycle:

SO I/26

> But you, divine one, you who sang to the end
> when the maenads attacked in scorned throng;
> you overcame their riot with order, sweet friend—
> out of destruction, arose your uplifting song.
>
> None there could hurt your head or your lyre
> no matter how fiercely they raged; all the sharp
> stones they flung at your heart, deep crier,
> softened to hear the strings of your harp.
>
> Furious, they finally smashed that clear window-sill
> yet your voice echoes on in birds and in trees
> in lions, and stones. There you sing still.
>
> O lost god! You inexhaustible trace!
> Only because you were scattered by enmities
> we are now the hearers, and speak in tongues
>
> charged with nature's grace.

This particular sonnet had always been a problem poem for me; it had seemed especially difficult to translate into my own language. Part of the "problem" is undoubtedly the subject of my transformed version—the rewriting forced by history, the recasting of the maenad's act of dismemberment in terms of racial conflict. Yet as I reflected on these things, another connection—even a momentary closure—surfaced, for the poem does bring me back home—to American history, to the way the fact and image of black and white are inextricably bound up with the figurations of life and death, right and wrong, justice and injustice in the United States.

SP II/9

> *Sing sacred smith, striding right through the storm*
> *of wasted word and fire-throwing fist;*
> *recast riot in pattern of the form*
> *rebuilding beauty from the ruin of terror's tryst.*
>
> *None there hit the nail on the head;*
> *no matter how many red*
> *lips primed the pale face of night,*
> *hot licking lips could only mark the spot.*
>
> *King cried when the foot caught in the chain*
> *forged in Hell, and the dark mouth ran*
> *like a masked man. Long livid fane*
> *of fire! My first lady's burning fan—*
>
> *because strife scatters our single sound*
> *we hear our barque split, and love*
> *run aground.*

I say the poem brought me back "home," but where, pray tell, is that? For while humankind is a house divided against itself; is a people, a land, a globe where black and white, red, yellow, and brown clash and kill, we are all—every single human being—homeless. For the earth is our home, and if we despoil it, if we fail to learn how to live and love our spiritual brothers and sisters on this mothership, we doom our race to oblivion. The hubris of man has always been great, but I wonder if the gulf of his forgetfulness has ever been so profound as it is at present—so deep and so wide.

~

7/3 Epilogue (On the Jet over the Atlantic)

Watching the faces, the many, many different faces, the strangeness of "human being" strikes me again. For it is clear that it is a peculiar form of consciousness; one species, and not the only kind. To the educated eye, what has been "the history of humankind" is but a small white sail set amidst a vast and swelling ocean of ever-shifting hues; a tiny black bird wheeling in a great blue sky.

On the surface, it looks as if the human being may do whatever he or she pleases with nature. The schoolboy's paper wings grow into the flying machine that shrinks the globe; the tight rope of the girl is straightened, stretched taut, and swung up to the top of the mountain so an electric car can carry her to her new sport; the man in the cab of the dozer on the Rhone pushes and heaps the Kalk at will. And yet, in the midst of all this, we have to ask: To what is this strange kind related? Is our association with the earth such a mercenary affair, is this great body naught but the food and fuel for the self-entertainment of this species? Or is there some deeper kinship between these stick figures and the great plain that we people like an army of ants? Is there nothing that keeps us in line—no art, no culture, no nature—that attunes us to the song lines of the land?

The magnificent, invisible presence of Nature hangs around us like a torn shroud. The great forms of rock, of sky, of sea: These are wrapped around every action of our kind; these are our morning dress, our evening gown; the hero's mantle and the bride's trousseau. It is at our peril that we cast them off; and yet we do, for we know not how to wear our divine wardrobe. The very race is bereaved—have we not just yesterday lost a favorite son?—and yet, half of our kind seems scarcely aware of the fact and go around in plain clothes when they should be draped in black; others make billboards of the news, and—fitted out like traveling salesmen—hawk the relics of his memory like so many bits of Fuller brush (buy, and you shall be cleansed forever); while still others go about in the grimmest of garb, mistaking the solemn robe of justice for the cloak of mourning. Where, where are those seekers well-appareled for the journey we must take, where the throngs of pilgrims to the wall of wailing women that—if we could but walk through it—might show us history's other side, the belly of the fish?

There are many good threads: the songs and symbols of many cultures, many voices. And yet too many of the lines that have tied us to each other, and to the earth, have been recast in iron and linked in chains; while the infinitely more delicate, silken snares of Love are ruthlessly snapped by the machines of power, by pompous priests and senseless schools. We enter an era of world-community having forgotten the art of communion, so that the Love that falls as rain in the starry night runs like lost mercury across the face of the earth. And how many still look for this miracle? How many hands devote themselves to the bulldozing of this metallic manna, this wor(l)d-wonder, back into one glistening globe we might hang round our necks like a precious gem? For when the dream droplets are gathered, they do make a pearl of great price; dispersed and detached, it is but acid rain.

Part II

New World

Joe Byrd Cemetery, Huntsville, Texas (burial ground of the unclaimed dead and executed) (Scott Langley)

5

Death Sentence:
The Case of Gary Graham

Houston, TX

STARRY NIGHT

Black boy's got a smile on his face
O Starry Night—
He don't know his Daddy gotta go
Where there ain't no skylight.

Black boy loved his Daddy real well—
Ran home after school;
Grand Jury say he whipped somebody
And that ain't cool.

So they gonna put that Daddy down—
That's the Golden Rule;
Yeah, they gonna send Black Man downtown
And Black Boy to finishing school.

Ain't nobody gonna dream day-glow
The night that Daddy dies
Cause there ain't gonna be a Star in Heaven
To help the next sun rise.

8/13 Houston, Texas

It is 3:00 p.m. Friday, August 13. I am standing in the lobby of the Texas Resource Center in Houston, Texas. Let me tell you why I'm here.

The end of the 30-day reprieve that short-circuited Gary Graham's scheduled execution happened to coincide with my July 4 return to the United States. One of the first things I did after arriving back in the U.S.A. was to inquire about the status of Graham's case. The decision in *Johnson v. Texas* was as close as they come: five judges on one side, four on the other. Unfortunately, close doesn't count in the Supreme Court. Johnson lost the case.

With *Johnson* decided, there was no longer any legal obstacle blocking Graham's execution. The state of Texas did not delay much:

147

I soon learned that Graham, as they say, "had another date"; was scheduled to be executed in Harris County at 12:01 a.m. August 17. I am here, then, for the final days, to witness (and perhaps take some small part in) the concerted legal and political effort to save Gary Graham from execution one more time.

~

The Texas Resource Center is the hideout of several lawyers (some from TRC itself, others with the Legal Defense Fund of the NAACP) who are now serving as Graham's counsel. It is this legal team that, after the dismissal of Graham's first court-appointed attorney, finally uncovered the mass of evidence testifying to Graham's innocence.

I am standing in the "waiting area" of the office—standing, because there is no place to sit. All available space is occupied by those peculiarly massive file cabinets one often finds in law offices. No matter—I am in good company here: Einstein, Ghandi, and Martin Luther King gaze at me from the wall. These are all men who dedicated their lives to discovering, and acting upon, the truth, no matter how long it took to find it, no matter how long it took to put it into play, and no matter how much it cost.

Inside, the TRC offices are buzzing. A press conference is taking place, and the lawyers are detailing the latest phase of the complex legal action. I learn that a decision on the *federal* habeas appeal should come down within the next few hours; a decision by the *state* district court could also come down anytime. I've walked into the midst of the action.

In the bare vestibule, I begin perusing a copy of the **COMPLAINT CONCERNING VIOLATION OF CIVIL RIGHTS** filed by TRC/LDF lawyers on behalf of Gary Graham.

On the merits, one might think that this *federal* action might have a real chance of success. The suit claims *systemic* error and bias in the state of Texas' administration of the death penalty. As I understand it, the 30-day rule precludes focus on the particulars of Graham's own case; if, however, the lawyers can prove that Graham's sentence is just one more instance of a state judicial *system* that is not meeting the requirements of (federal) constitutional law, then Graham, and others, could obtain relief. The federal court is the appropriate body for such an action, since the LDF/TCR lawyers are effectively asking the federal judiciary to review state operations. In this case that means examining the record for evidence of *systematic racial bias in capital law,* and (perhaps yet more importantly) a system that effectively prevents counsel from providing adequate legal assistance to indigent defendants. The complaint begins:

> Gary Graham, a young black man, is scheduled to be executed by the State of Texas . . . for a crime he did not commit. Mr. Graham's case is illustrative of two grave constitutional flaws in the administration of the death penalty in Texas which call for a thorough investigation by the United States Department of Justice:
>
> (1) gross racial disparity in sentencing and (2) systemic deprivation of effective assistance of counsel for poor people.

Without examining any of the details of the brief, let's look at some of the *historical background* that will help provide a context for understanding the wider significance of the Graham case.

(1) gross racial disparity in sentencing

There are a number of reasons why Graham is on death row. His race, and—still more importantly, Bobby Lambert's—almost certainly among them. There is, in fact, *a long and historic bond between capital jurisprudence and questions of racial discrimination,* a history inscribed, most signally, in the Supreme Court record. Indeed, Graham's own case has already been the occasion for one of the more recent, and provocative, entries in that record.

Justice Clarence Thomas cast a deciding vote in the *Johnson v. Texas* case, and that was not the first time that the sole Black justice sitting on the Supreme Court had cleared the way for Graham's execution. In an earlier phase of Graham's own case—*Graham v. Collins* (1991)— Justice Thomas had played an identical role, providing the margin of difference in a five to four decision. Moreover, in that case—not content merely to sign the majority opinion—Thomas filed a concurring opinion, reviewing certain elements of capital jurisprudence since the watershed *Furman v. Georgia* decision of 1972. The Thomas opinion in *Graham v. Collins* must surely contain some of the most (and here I borrow Justice John Paul Stevens' carefully selected word) "remarkable" reasoning bound into the annals of Supreme Court law.

Thomas' opinion begins by evoking the social atmosphere of the *Furman* decision:

> It is important to recall what motivated Members of the Court at the genesis of our modern capital punishment case law. *Furman vs. Georgia* was decided in an atmosphere suffused with concern about race bias in the administration of the death penalty—particularly in Southern States, and most particularly in rape cases. Lucious Jackson was a 21-year-old black man sentenced to death by Georgia for raping a white woman. Elmer Branch was sentenced to death by Texas for the rape of 65-year-old white widow. Willie Henry Furman faced the death penalty in Georgia for unintentionally killing a white homeowner during a burglary . . . Citing studies and reports suggesting that the death sentence was disproportionately imposed and carried out on the poor, the Negro, and members of unpopular groups, especially in cases of rape, Justice William O. Douglas concluded that:
>
> "The discretion of judges and juries in imposing the death penalty enables the penalty to be selectively applied, feeding prejudices against the accused if he is poor and despised, and lacking political clout, or if he is a member of a suspect or

unpopular minority, and saving those who by social position may be in a more protected position."

Thomas' opinion then cites similar passages from the opinions of Justices Thurgood Marshall and Potter Stewart. Since Graham himself is represented, in large part, by lawyers from the LDF, Thomas' next remark supplies another index of the historic connection between Graham's case and *Furman*:

> The unquestionable importance of race in Furman is reflected in the fact that three of the original four petitioners in the Furman cases were represented by the NAACP Legal Defense and Educational Fund, Inc.

The initial section of Thomas' lengthy opinion concludes:

> In sum, the Court concluded that in a standardless sentencing scheme there was no "rational basis," as Justice Brennan put it, to distinguish "the few who die from the many who go to prison." It cannot be doubted that behind the Court's condemnation of unguided discretion lay the specter of racial prejudice—the paradigmatic capricious and irrational sentencing factor.

It should be noted that in the *Graham v. Collins* phase of the case, the counsel for the defense was *not* contending racial discrimination had disturbed due process, but rather that Texas statute did not allow sufficient consideration of mitigating factors (here, primarily youth, as in *Johnson*) that might move a jury to bypass the death penalty in favor of a lesser sentence. Nonetheless, Thomas' opinion effectively evokes the wider social and historical context within which Graham's case must ultimately be viewed. The civil rights concerns evoked by Thomas as the *background* of *Graham v. Collins,* are *foregrounded* in the pending phase of the case, the complaint recently filed by LDF and TRC lawyers currently before the court.

Tomorrow, I understand, I will have a chance to hear Richard Burr, an LDF lawyer, detail the substance of the argument's complaints. For now, let us return to the Thomas opinion and the historical context it supplies.

Although *Graham v. Collins* did not specifically ask the court to consider evidence of racial bias, one might have expected that Justice Thomas—who took such pains to evoke the racial background of Furman in his opinion—might have recognized the persistence of the paradigmatic "capricious and irrational sentencing factor," and effectively weighed in *against* the death sentence, in Graham's case and in general. But such was not the case. In the rest of the *Graham v. Collins* opinion, Thomas makes perfectly clear that he supports the death penalty in principle and believes that the problem of racial bias in sentencing can be best dealt with by imposing rigid sentencing schemas that radically restrict the discretion of judge and juries in sentencing. The extreme of this kind of *pro forma* "rationality" would be the mandatory sentence: If such and such a crime is committed, the offender—regardless of circumstances—will be punished by death. Though the court has rejected such schemas as too inflexible, Thomas indicates that he might well favor them.

On the surface, the rigid rule of fixed sentencing schemas may well appear a "reasonable" solution to race discrimination. But Thomas' own opinion in *Graham v. Collins* displays the irrationality that so easily pervades abstracted logic.

The bulk of Thomas' opinion registers his disagreement with the Supreme Court's decision in *Penry v. Lynaugh,* in which the court held that the defendant's mental retardation must be taken into special consideration in sentencing. Because it broadens the *discretion* of judge and jury in sentencing, Thomas sees *Penry* as a threat to progress represented by *Furman.* His opinion concludes with this excited statement:

Every month, defendants who claim a special victimization file with this Court petitions for certiorari that ask us to declare that some new class of evidence has mitigating relevance "beyond the scope" of the State's sentencing criteria. It may be evidence of voluntary intoxication or of drug use. Or even—astonishingly—evidence that the defendant suffers from chronic "antisocial personality disorder"—that is, that he is a sociopath . . . We cannot carry on such a business, which makes a mockery of the concerns about racial discrimination that inspired our decision in *Furman*.

As Justice Stevens points out, Thomas' logic here is strange indeed:

Justice Thomas . . . is surely correct the concern about racial discrimination played a significant role in the development of our modern capital sentencing jurisprudence . . . Where I cannot agree with Justice Thomas is in the remarkable suggestion that the Court's decision *Penry v. Lynaugh* . . . somehow threatens what progress we have made in eliminating racial discrimination and other arbitrary considerations from the capital sentencing determination . . . Nothing in Justice Thomas' opinion explains why the requirement that sentencing decisions be based on *relevant* mitigating evidence, as applied by *Penry*, increases the risk that those decisions will be based on the *irrelevant* factor of race. More specifically, I do not see how permitting full consideration of a defendant's mental retardation and history of childhood abuse, as in *Penry*, or of a defendant's youth, as in this case, in any way increases the risk of race-based or otherwise arbitrary decision-making.

These are excerpts from the text of the decision, but the subtext is not, I think, hard to read. Why does Thomas invoke Furman, so effectively evoking *the historic connection between capital jurisprudence and racial discrimination*? Because (as the LDF's current suit alleges) the problem of racial discrimination in capital sentencing is not merely "history" but pervasive, too, in the present day. The recognition that the institution of capital punishment continues to be contaminated by racial bias accounts for the widespread opposition to it in the black community. As the language of his opinion shows, Justice Thomas—the sole black justice and heir of Thurgood Marshall's seat—*could not be unaware of the special racial valence of his decision in* Graham v. Collins. His opinion reveals the twisted logic by which he sought to reconcile two irreconcilable facts: support for the death penalty and recognition of the racial discrimination that has long infected the institution. The elaborate apparatus of his argument can be seen as a cover for the simple fact that it was *not* the court's decision to mandate due consideration of Penry's mental retardation that threatened the progress made by *Furman,* but an African-American Supreme Court justice's own willingness to lend his decisive support to the sentence of death, condemning—quite possibly—a young (probably innocent) black man to die at the hands of the state. The notion that abstractly "rational" sentencing schemes could effectively erase the residue of race from the history (and futurity) of capital jurisprudence—squeeze blood color out of the machinations of the society—recalls the logic parodied in another, earlier passage of American history:

. . . one day Ringo slipped off and went to town and came back and he looked at me with his eyes rolling a little.

"Do you know what I ain't" he said.

"What?" I said.

"I ain't a nigger any more. I done been abolished."

Then I asked him what he was, if he wasn't a nigger anymore and he showed me what he had in his hand. It was a new scrip dollar; it was drawn on the United States, Resident Treasurer, Yoknapatawpha County, Mississippi, and signed "Cassius Q. Benbow, Acting Marshal" in a neat clerk's hand, with a big sprawling X under it.

"Cassius Q. Benbow?" I said.

"*Correct*," *Ringo said*. "*Uncle Cash that druv the Benbow carriage twell he run off with the Yankees two years ago. He back now and he gonter be elected Marshal of Jefferson. That's what Marse John and the other white folks is so busy about*."

"*A nigger?*" *I said*. "*A nigger?*"

"*No*," *Ringo said*. "*They ain't no more niggers, in Jefferson nor nowhere else*."

(2) *systemic deprivation of effective assistance of counsel for poor people*

While race is almost certainly one of the reasons Gary Graham is on death row, yet it is not necessarily the most important one. That honor is probably reserved for the second factor mentioned in the complaint brought by Graham's lawyers: what the law calls "ineffective assistance of counsel." Since there was no money on hand to fund Graham's defense, neither was there a Robert Shapiro or Johnny Cochrane on the scene; instead, Gary Graham had to make to do with whatever defense counsel the state might provide him. But Graham's federal complaint argues that the Texas system illegally impairs his (and other indigent defendant's) constitutional right to due counsel. In this instance, the complaint itself supplies the relevant historical background, so I quote from it at length:

> The Supreme Court has recognized that the right to counsel under the sixth and fourteenth amendments can be denied in two distinctly different ways. Counsel may perform deficiently, making mistakes inadvertently or through ill-informed decisions that deprive their clients of the reasonable professional assistance to which they are entitled . . . On the other hand, counsel may find themselves forced to represent clients under conditions that make it impossible to provide effective representation, no matter how ably they perform. Though counsel is not at fault in these circumstances, the

right to the assistance of counsel is vitiated just as much as if counsel performed inadequately.

Among the cases which the Supreme Court has used to illustrate the circumstantial deprivation of counsel is the case of the Scottsboro Boys, reported as Powell v. Alabama, 287 U.S. 45 (1932). Seven young black men traveling through Alabama on a train were charged with the rape of two young white women. The trial court appointed *all* the members of the local bar to represent the defendants . . . Because no one felt any sense of responsibility, nothing was done to prepare for trial. On the day of trial, a lawyer from Tennessee appeared specially to raise the defendants' interest in having the assistance of counsel; over his protest, he was appointed, and the trial commenced. Faced with the claim that, despite this lawyer's efforts, the defendants had been denied the assistance of counsel, "the court did not examine the actual performance of counsel at trial, but instead concluded that under these circumstances the likelihood that counsel could have performed as an effective adversary was so remote as to have made the trial inherently unfair."

Although counsel who represent poor people charged with capital murder in Texas are not often forced to represent their clients in circumstances similar to those [in the case of the Scottsboro boys], they are often forced to represent their clients under conditions that make it virtually impossible to provide effective representation . . .

It is this problem—a modern-day variation on the denial of the assistance of counsel that so troubled the Court in *Powell*—to which we direct the [Justice] Department's attention. Its tragic consequences are not better illustrated than in the case of the complainant, Gary Graham, who was convicted and sentenced to death for a crime that it is now increasingly clear he did not commit.

The news conference has broken up some time ago; people are milling about the TRC offices. I am just about to begin reading section IIA of the brief, to understand how *"The System Used by Texas to Provide Counsel to Poor People Charged with Capital Crimes Makes It Extremely Difficult for Counsel to Provide Effective Representation"* when the entire atmosphere of the office suddenly stills and darkens. All too soon, the message is clear: Whatever *I* may think of the argument in my hands, the LDF/TRC lawyers have *not* succeeded in convincing the court to follow the precedent of the Scottsboro boys, to move to avert the "tragic consequences" scheduled to take place just a few days from now. Graham's civil rights suit, his federal complaint, has been *rejected*—dismissed, without so much as a hearing being granted to consider his complaint.

Tired and dazed, I walk over to the rather makeshift office of the Gary Graham Coalition offices, just a few doors down from TRC. The negative result has momentarily overwhelmed one of the coalition's founders. From the next room, one can hear her bitter, almost hysterical weeping. And then—intermittently—the calm, comforting voice of another sister who seeks, in vain, to find words to stem the tide of grief and despair.

Now there is only the comparatively weak *state* court action— one the lawyers have little faith in standing between Graham and execution.

Another one of the coalition's leaders—a tall, self-possessed black man with the distinctive name of Reverend Jew Don Boney—comes into the coalition offices. Reverend Boney and Susan Dillow—a black activist minister and a soft-spoken public accountant whose political styles are a study in contrast—have spearheaded much of the political action on Graham's behalf. Now, it seems, some documents must be delivered immediately— within the next few minutes—some miles away, and the courier is uncertain of directions. A stranger to the town, I nevertheless have my city map on hand and give it to Reverend Bony. We do not exchange names; words seem vain in this darkness. I feel myself cast in the midst of a mute tragic drama. I do not know my part.

Next door, the Greek chorus continues to sound.

~

The decision in the federal court was dismaying, but not surprising. At this late date, all Graham's legal options are seriously hampered by the 30-day rule, for the greatest strength in his particular case does in fact rest primarily upon new evidence—evidence the court has decided it is in no position to review.

Yet the courts are not the only source of potential relief: That may also, in exceptional cases, come from the executive branch in the form of *clemency*. If the courts do not act to prevent a patent miscarriage of justice in a given state, the governor (or somebody answerable to the executive branch) can. If the record casts the guilt of the accused in grave doubt, the governor or appointed delegates can exercise the power of clemency, can grant a full pardon, or commute the death penalty to life imprisonment or some other penalty.

In the Graham case, seeking relief through clemency has one great advantage: There is no *law* preventing rational human beings from actually reviewing all available evidence, all facts that might confirm or refute the guilt of the accused. Relief through clemency has one great *disadvantage*: There is no law requiring or establishing procedures for such review. Clemency is a discretionary measure. Dependent, most usually, upon the reason, common sense, and humanity of the governor, its primary purpose is to provide a safety valve that can rectify manifest malfunctions in the machinery of justice.

The discretionary character of clemency explains why Graham's lawyers are not optimistic about the suit filed before the *state* court. The suit asks the court, in effect, to guarantee Graham some kind of "due process" in connection with clemency review proceedings. This requires that the court treat clemency review as an essentially juridical process, a perspective that has a fairly strong, but by no means unequivocal, basis in precedent.

Technicalities aside, given the strength of the exculpatory evidence in Graham's case, one might well *hope* that clemency would provide relief that the courts would not; would, at the least, short-circuit the execution, rescind the penalty of death. Given the facts of the case, that would be a reasonable expectation in a rational, in a civilized world.

But it does not take long to find out that the political life here is anything but civilized or rational. This is, after all, Harris County, Texas: death penalty capital of the world.

What is it like to enter here? Imagine yourself walking into a Roman amphitheater—not, *now,* to watch sporting *razeteurs* run the *course libre*—but *then,* way back then, when armed gladiators killed wild beasts, Christians, or each other. Imagine yourself there, in the thick of the roaring crowd. Look up now, see the Doric or Corinthian columns (melt them in your mind and put up those of a modern courthouse, or a state mansion). Still amidst the roar, imagine Cicero on the steps, speaking for liberty. His periods are not quite so long as they were—though still eloquent, his rhythms are different. He raises his voice, striving to be heard above the crowd—another brother is thrown into the ring.

The clemency process in Texas is—to say the least—confusing. Unlike the process in many other states, it is not directly vested in the person of the governor. She does have the autonomous power to grant one 30-day reprieve (a power Ann Richards did exercise to avert Graham's first execution), but more permanent decisions are vested in the Texas Board of Pardon and Paroles. It is this 17-member body that could, for instance, decide that—in light of newly discovered evidence, which the board, *unlike* the courts, can officially review—Graham's guilt had *not* been proved beyond a reasonable doubt. The Texas

Board of Pardon and Paroles *could* do that, but won't—at least, not right away. In fact, the Texas board won't even look at Graham's case unless, perhaps, the governor (who appoints the members and naturally retains considerable clout with the board) asks it to; or (and here is a bit of irony) unless it is ultimately required to do so by the fickle hand of "law."

To understand the politics of this situation, it is necessary to know a little bit about the Texas board.

The board's primary responsibility is administration of parole. In fact, it might well be fair to say that, historically, the board itself has perceived that as its sole role. Though it does technically possess the power to grant clemency, it has not, historically, chosen to the exercise that power; as a matter of fact, the Texas board has never sought fit to pardon anyone. It is, indeed, the Texas Board of Pardon and Parole in name only; in fact, it is the Texas Board of Parole.

Why? Is it because no plausible candidates for pardon have come through the Texas system? There are other, more likely explanations for the board's (perfect) record, such as the rather remarkable truth that there have been *no formal guidelines set down for the processes of pardon review.* The board has been free to do whatever it did or didn't feel like. Predictably, most of the time, this has meant doing—absolutely nothing.

But the case of Gary Graham is a little different. On account of the publicity Graham's case has received; on account of the shadow of doubt cast upon his guilt—doubt that led to Governor Richard's initial 30-day reprieve—the board did meet to decide whether or not it would review Graham's case. But since there is no procedure establishing guidelines for the making of such decisions —no procedure, for instance, for the consideration of exculpatory evidence—the board did not feel compelled to do anything like call witnesses or compile a complete evidentiary record. It did review some written evidence (affidavits and the like) before deciding that there was no compelling reason to question the guilty verdict in the Graham trial; no reason even to review the evidence, even to consider clemency in this case.

But fate moves in strange ways. The patent irrationality (one might say "capriciousness") of the board's operation combined with a recent Supreme Court decision to open a legal loophole just large enough for Graham's life to walk through.

4:00 p.m. There is a commotion down the hall at the TRC. Someone comes running into the coalition offices, waving white papers. Evidently, the news is good this time. The case no one thought would make a difference does. A stay of execution has come down through the District Court. The chorus stops. For one all-too-brief moment, despair is transformed into relief and joy. For the time being, a life (we will not say a soul; that was never in danger) has been saved.

You will want to know the substance of the District Court Judge Pete Lowry's decision in cause No. 93-08624, Gary Graham v. Texas Board of Pardons and Paroles, et. al. As is the general rule in law, a precedent stemming from another case proved pivotal in Graham's; in this case, *Herrera v. Collins*. Like Graham, Herrara had been accused and convicted of capital murder and was scheduled for execution when new evidence emerged in his case. On the face of it, Herrara's new evidence seems less trustworthy or compelling than in Graham's case, but the quality of Herrara's evidence is not so important to us now as the procedure established to review it. Herrara asked the Supreme Court to order the lower court responsible for his conviction to rehear his case, admitting the newly discovered evidence. In a crucial decision, however, the Supreme Court *rejected* Herrara's plea. Writing for the majority, Justice William Rehnquist asserted that so long as the initial trial had been just and free of legal error, there was no standing obligation to hear new evidence. *However* (and this is crucial), Rehnquist stressed the decision did *not* foreclose the patent necessity for *some* mechanism of post-trial review. That function, wrote Rehnquist, was traditionally filled by executive *clemency*:

> Executive clemency has provided the 'fail safe' in our criminal justice system. It is an unalterable fact that our judicial system, like the human beings that administer it, is fallible. But history is replete with examples of wrongfully convicted persons who have been pardoned in the wake of after-discovered evidence establishing their innocence.

After elaborating why federal habeas corpus relief was not appropriate in the case, Rehnquist continues:

> This is not to say, however, that petitioner is not left without a forum to raise his actual innocence claim . . . Clemency is deeply rooted in our Anglo-American tradition of law, and is the historic remedy for preventing miscarriages of justice where judicial process has been exhausted.

These passages, cited in District Court Judge's Pete Lowry's decision, supplied Lowry with legal rationale for holding that—given the weight of the evidence in Graham's own case—*he is <u>constitutionally</u> entitled to an <u>evidentiary, due course of law hearing</u> before the Texas Board of Pardon and Paroles;* and that his *execution must be stayed* until such time as such review has been granted. Lowry's opinion reads:

> My ruling in this case is based upon the Herrera Court's assertion that the Texas clemency process is the "fail safe" that prevents the execution of an innocent person. By declining to exercise federal judicial control in cases involving claims of actual innocence based on newly discovered evidence, the Supreme Court deferred to the State of Texas the right and the responsibility to exercise that control. The State, therefore, must exercise that right and responsibility, and it can only do so through the process of executive clemency.

Here is the half-biblical, half-bureaucratic language of the law:

TEMPORARY INJUNCTION

BE IT REMEMBERED on the 27th day of July, 1993, came on to be heard the motion of Gary Graham, Plaintiff in this cause, for a temporary injunction, as prayed for in his petition and verified motion. Notice was given to, and received by, all parties; and the parties appeared by their attorneys.

The Court, having considered the arguments and pleadings of counsel, as well as the evidence in the case, finds and concludes, as follows: that Plaintiff will probably prevail on the trial of this cause; that Defendants Texas Board of Pardons and Paroles . . . and all those acting in concert with them intend to refuse to grant Plaintiff a due course of law hearing on his post-conviction claim of innocence . . . and thereby intend to allow the execution of Plaintiff to occur on August 17, 1993 before the Court can render judgment in this cause . . . that, unless Defendants . . . and all those acting in concert with them are deterred, restrained, and enjoined from carrying out that intention, Plaintiff will be completely without any remedy at law and will suffer death.

IT IS THEREFORE ORDERED that Defendants Texas Board of Pardons and Paroles . . . and all those acting in concert with them, be, and hereby are commanded forthwith to grant Plaintiff a due course of law hearing on his post-conviction claim of innocence . . . or, failing that, they are commanded to issue a *temporary stay of such execution* until a hearing . . . is held on Plaintiff's post-judgment evidence of his claim of innocence or until judgment in this cause is entered by this Court.

IT IS FURTHER ORDERED THAT, should Defendants Texas Board of Pardons and Paroles and . . . all those acting in concert with them, grant Plaintiff a due course of law hearing on his claim of innocence . . . such Defendants and persons shall assure that due course of law hearing will utilize the following procedures:

1. A hearing before an impartial officer;

2. The right to confront evidence and witnesses against him and to cross-examine them during such hearing;

3. The right to a written summary of the findings and decision of the hearing officer;

4. The right to be represented by counsel during such hearing;

5. The right to have the hearing transcribed by a court reporter;

6. The right to adequately prepare for such a hearing.

Thus was the good news delivered: Perhaps the evidence of Graham's innocence would, at last, at least be spoken, if not heard.

~

Having been led, as we believe, by the spirit of God . . . we do now, in the presence of God and this assembly, most solemnly and joyfully enter into covenant with one another as one body in Christ. We engage therefore by the aid of the Holy Spirit, to walk together in Christian love . . . .

—*First Missionary Baptist Church,*
Barrett Station, Texas

In the evening, I drive out to a small church in Barrett Station, Crosby (a largely black "suburb" of Houston) to attend a gospel fundraiser organized by the Gary Graham coalition. As I walk up to the church, two newsmen (the camera, of course, is the give away) are conversing in German just outside. This is not really surprising, since I already know that Graham's case has received quite a lot of international attention. Citizens and politicians from many countries have signed petitions in support of his cause. As these news cameras attest, it is not only the citizens of this country who have a spiritual interest in what happens to Gary Graham. His is a case that reveals something about who we are in the eyes of the world.

Performing my duty as a "journalist," I ask my continental colleagues for their thoughts about the Graham case. In between tugs at a recalcitrant camera, they express the gist of the civilized world's reaction to the Graham trial: They are absolutely astonished that the United States would *convict* and proceed to *kill* a human being on the basis of such slim evidence. Of course, still more egregious human rights abuses take place routinely in other parts of the world, but this, in *America?*

I am warmed by their sympathies; I only wish the disbelief that shines in their eyes were reflected in my own.

The church at Barrett Station is no Vatican, no towering Palace of the Popes. After entering the thoroughly nondescript building, I take a seat on one of the long wooden pews. There are a good number of people in the church already; by the end of the evening, it will be largely full. Most—but by no means all—of the faces are black. The atmosphere is warm and quite welcoming. After a few minutes, I feel more at home here than I ever did in the reform temple of my youth, where all the words and gestures were inexpressive and foreign, and all the eyes were windows with suburban curtains drawn.

But here, all are gathered in the shadow of death, and so—paradoxically—everything feels vital and alive. As I sit calmly in the pew, absorbing the atmosphere, even time and place take on a certain, almost palpable pungency. For time and space are not really (as one German philosopher maintained) abstract categories of perception, but plastic molds themselves shaped and tinted by the experience poured into them. Momentarily, my mind wanders back to the cathedral at Chartres; there are no stained glass windows here, to be sure, but the interior is nonetheless full of color, distinguished by the light shining from the dancing shades of many eyes.

After some time, the evening's events begin. Reverend Tommy Johnson, the minister of the church, starts with a brief address. Naturally, the good news about the stay of execution (known by most already) is shared. Thanks are offered, and the furtherance of God's grace prayed for in silence.

As I participate in these goings-on, the truth that Gary Graham's case is about more, much more, than one man's life, comes more deeply home to me, entering into the body of my being. I knew from the first that there were profound principles involved; not merely political and religious principles, but—perhaps—the very principle of religion and politics per se as such come down to us from certain treasured traditions. But the mind's grasp of such matters is never quite the same as their physical manifestation, their *incorporation* in the body of a people or a faith. The spirit is not what it is until it passes like an electric current through a circuit of linked hands.

Several other individuals associated, one way or another, with Graham's cause have spoken briefly. But now the preaching starts—not, interestingly enough, with the words of a Christian minister, but rather with those of Minister Robert Muhammad, spiritual head of the Nation of Islam in the Houston area. It may be somewhat unusual to hear a Muslim preach in church, but Muslims have been supportive of Graham's cause; later in the evening, Reverend Boney will thank them for contributing time and resources "when there wasn't a Christian in sight."

In any event, once Robert Muhammed began to speak, creedal difference did not stand in the way of religious education. He had arrived late and, as he said, needed time to "warm" to his topic, but by the time he had finished telling us, in 15 different, equally provocative ways that "Jesus may be the answer, but *what is the question*" his mixture of Gospel preaching and Socratic dialogue had me actually *thinking* about matters that are seldom touched upon in church or anywhere else. Then Reverend Jew Don Boney picked up where Minister Muhammad left off, speaking of the threefold constitution of the true Christian who—according to his scriptural text—must combine in himself the attributes of *King, Priest* and *Prophet*. And then the music—the gospel singing—began . . .

"Holy Ghost come on down, we can do nothing until he comes . . . Holy Ghost come on down; we can do nothing until he comes . . .

. . . the musical phrases repeated over and over by the swelling chorus of voices, the rhythm marked by the host of clapping hands.

The evening ended with another quintessentially "relevant" phrase. Unfortunately, I cannot sing you the song. But even a writer can cite the text, pop the question:

"Where are all the Christians?"

And—so long as we are in a gospel mood—let me read to you a letter I wrote in the springtime of this year.

May 26, 1993

Dear Hillary Rodham-Clinton (*President Clinton, Governor Richards*)

I am writing you in behalf of Gary Graham, beseeching you, in the name of mercy, love, and the sacred memory of our blessed mother and her true son, to seek the pardon of this man's life.

I write to *you,* in particular, Hillary Rodham Clinton, on account of an article I read about a speech you gave in Texas. The writer of that piece was clearly cynical about your yearnings for spiritual renewal, but any unspoiled soul could not but be warmed by the intelligent and compassionate nature that shone through the story's sardonic surface like a pearl of great price.

That pearl is the beauty of our human being, a precious jewel that has fallen by the wayside of history, and now lies so deeply buried in the grime of our fearful selfforgetfulness, that to believe in truth, beauty, and the forgiveness of sins is nigh a crime in our politic society. And to believe—*to know*—the truth of these things is something quite different from the mouthing of creeds that characterizes too much of what passes for religion today. Those in power who *do* honor the truths of the heart are under sacred obligation to act in their behalf wherever possible; for only so does the real benevolence of the spirit become manifest; only so is that lost pearl polished, and found.

The *"politics of meaning"* can have no meaning unless this be founded upon the rock of living insight: spiritual perception into the truths of the human soul, and the relation of those truths to the ongoing course of human affairs. Without such animating vision—which springs from transforming contemplation of perennial truths—religion degenerates into rote rehearsal and mere moralism; codes of conduct that seek to *impose* norms and values because it has lost the light that convinces by the great suasions of love, and truth's living example.

But the movement of grace in our lives (and living participation in spiritual truths is always a kind of grace) has its ethical requisites: namely, the punctual discharge of those spiritual duties we are appointed and empowered to perform. And it is in connection with this order of obligation that I would like, for a moment, to consider with you the case of Gary Graham. For the *pardon* of this man's life— together with the *understanding* of the spiritual reason and necessity for that act—is one of the inaugural acts required to usher in a new era in the life of this nation: one premised upon the promise of love, and presided over—not by partisan politics—but by the bonds of brothers and sisters, the spiritual constitution that frames us all as true friends, and creates anew the covenant of our kind.

Such words should not be spoken lightly. Who, you will ask, has the authority to speak in the name of the spirit? There are many answers to that question—some as simple as the ray of light in early morning, others complex as entire cities of scripture. But I shall not speak to that issue here, but merely answer back with another, more pressing question—who, we should ask, has the *right* to condemn a man to die?

For this is an act of immense consequence, an enormous presumption of authority. And I would suggest to you that the American state should in no wise presume to such authority, and that, indeed, to do so constitutes a fateful trespass of spiritual boundaries—one that effectively *enslaves* this nation to the cycle of violence and retribution that gnaws at its spiritual heart like the eagle at the liver of Prometheus.

Of course the death penalty is—shall we say—popular. Many say: "this man *killed*, let him die for his deed. We can find ample precedent for such judgment in the Bible itself; how long are we going to allow people of this nation to get away with murder? We have had enough of the reign of terror that rules our streets; enough of the lawlessness of youth; enough of the milk-livered liberalism that makes a policy of pardoning criminals, and a platform of sanctioning social deviance. Let the criminal who kills know that act forfeits his life: this is just, this secures our society. We do not want to pamper the guilty, but to protect the innocent; we do not want to live in a world of fear."

But I would suggest to you that such reasoning shall never achieve the peace it craves, but can only confirm and perpetuate the fear that guts the spiritual house of this land. I ask you, for a moment, to look at this issue—not from the narrow, time-bound point of view that considers truth a kind of trench-warfare, but in the light of spiritual reason, and most especially, the religious truth of Christ, and the lesson of his great sacrifice.

It has been said that America is a "Christian nation" and while many, for good reason, took issue with that statement, it is true that there are many, many Americans who do profess the Christian faith. And yet, it does not take a saint to see that *no* country that routinely condemns human beings to die can ever be a "Christian" nation, for the sentence of death—born of fear and vengeance—violates the memory of the body and the blood of Christ. For if we follow the lines of spiritual logic, we will be led to one, inescapable conclusion; namely, that capital punishment is the symbolic negation of the life-in-death of Christ, the *contradiction* of the crucifixion. Or, to put the same truth in more artistic terms, we may say that the *prospect* of state-sanctioned execution is the cruel caricature of the master's glorious portrait; one that literally *disfigures* the face of our first friend beyond . . . belief.

To see these things is not so difficult or abstruse a matter; one must merely scan the historical record with an open eye, and colorful pen. Christ was killed by an angry mob; his murder finally sanctioned by the Roman state. And it is clear that Christ forgave those who sinned against him—including those who killed him—even before he climbed the cross. The meaning of his death cannot be sundered from that forgiveness. If Christ had harbored retribution in his soul, his heart would not be the sacred salve it is for those who abide in him, but another ordinary organ pumped by fear, another animal function ruled by instinct, another abacus of analysis reasoning its own selfish needs.

But Christ lived and thought differently. His supreme sacrifice says: "even those who crucify me, even you, soldier with your spear—I do not condemn you; you know not what you do. And on that day you do know—on that blessed day when you do see me aright, you shall repent of what you have done, and you will be pardoned, for the gateway to God's love is never shut. This broken body is the threshold of that love, these outstretched arms, that open door."

Capital punishment swings shut that door. Two thousand years after Christ, this "civilized" even so-called "Christian" nation continues to play Pilate and the vengeful mob, routinely condemning sundry individuals to die, even though each and every human being— including those who have strayed so far as to take another human life—have been made potentially incorporate in Christ; forever enfranchised, by his sacrifice, in the infinite mercy of the mind of God. To condemn any body and soul to guilt without repeal (a fair reading of capital punishment) is to deny their participation in the spirit of the Christ, and so, inevitably, to deny Christ himself. For if the Son gave his life so we might live, he lives his new life not in some celestial palace replete with harps and little white angels, but through us, and the terms of our acceptance of his great gift.

And so you will understand that I would not want to be informed that the "official functions" of the state in no wise unjustly infringe upon Gary Graham's "spiritual life," that indeed, he may still be (as they say) "saved" before the date of his state-appointed death. Such reasoning might do for the feudal ages, but will hardly serve for an American government that strives for a more enlightened mode of rule, a *body politic* that would assume *spiritual responsibility* for its own actions. It is positively monstrous to employ the "consolations" of "religion" to excuse state-sanctioned violence—as if "*heaven*" and *the spirit in which we conduct our earthly affairs* were entirely different realms; as if the form of "our Father in heaven" happily cohabited with the canon of cruelty on Earth.

Each and every one of our state-authorized executions is a spiritual crime that repeats, rather than repeals, the original murder; a tragic act of collective hubris, in which the fear-driven body politic and the publicity-driven state arrogates (incredibly!) to itself the species of infallibility and perfection proper only to God, and never to man. Only that being innocent of all crime, and omniscient in judgment, has spiritual authority to issue last judgments— that judgment without repeal which capital punishment stands for *here*.

Once we have published these truths, we cannot but draw from them the gravest conclusions. Given to see what has been said here, we are given to know, as well, that the official institution of capital punishment, and the numerous executions carried out by law, actually possesses the power to negate—render *null* and *void*—the spiritual efficacy of the crucifixion, the death that is the central event in the life of Christ.

How can this be? Is not such a statement blasphemy? Perhaps I shall be burned at the stake for it——God knows the church itself has, historically, been one of the greatest offenders on this score. But, to the innocent and intelligent heart, the spiritual logic is straightforward enough. The sacrifice of the Christ is made good when it is *accepted*, not when it is *rejected*; such acceptance, however, cannot take the form of a blind belief or mindless assent, but is rather an act of *felt understanding* that stems from the spiritual vision and consent of the heart, and which vouchsafes us actual participation in the spirit of the Christ.

To arrive at that understanding is—to be sure—no easy matter. But we can see and say this much: that the event of the crucifixion dramatizes the sacredness of death, showing us that death, symbolically construed (and the symbolic and the literal coincide in Christ) is not the end of life, but rather its beginning; the threshold, that is, to a new life in God. Or, we might say (with Rilke), that truly considered, we are here shown that death is not the opposite or negation of life, but rather its *complement,* the other side of the same coin that first allows us to estimate the true value of the face we see . . . as if for the first time.

But the ghastly caricature of Christ's divine sacrifice that is capital punishment *profanes death,* blinding our eyes to these deeper spiritual meanings. The death sentence is like a silent movie poster pasted over the divine picture of the Christ; one that makes it impossible for us to *read* the message printed there. For this whispered sentence purports to put the power of death into the hands of man, and makes of it—not a new beginning *within* life itself, but the fearful terminal of time, robbing it of the *redemptive function* hidden in its inscrutable darkness. Thus, the people and nations who lend *consent* to the penalty of death are thereby inevitably rendered *unreceptive* to the true meaning of the crucifixion.

Pledging ourselves to live by laws framed by human fear, rather than divine love, we condemn ourselves to wander indefinitely in the spiritual wasteland that is the modern world.

Let us, for a moment, take prophecy seriously, and suppose the spirit of Christ might come to us again. How, we may well ask, could we conceivably *see* him with such dirty glass covering our eyes? If we want his spirit to come to us, if we ourselves wish to enter the kingdom of kindness, must we not prepare ourselves, and do our homework a little better, must we not show that we, as a people, have studied our history lessons, and made application of it to our laws and mores? The cross sits proudly upon the steeple of the church, but what good will all our prayers perform if this awful sentence hovers over our land like a ghostly spectre of Roman times, profaning the principles for which the true Son stands?

And so I ask you: the citizen who goes to mass in the morning, and signs Gary Graham's death warrant on June the 3rd (for every hand that does not wave in his defense must be complicit in this crime): will this continue to be the character of our kind, the type of our American-style "Christian" "religion"? How long will we run the cycle of fear and terror like white mice in a cage—afraid to walk out, because we do not trust the hand that opens the door? How long will we live in a land where *power* has no *love,* and *love* no *power,* and the Spirit of the Son is an empty, almost effaced sign?

And so I ask you, Hillary Rodham Clinton—and through you, *you,* President Clinton and, *you,* Governor Richards, to have the courage to perform a true spiritual duty, and to work to secure the life of Gary Graham—a deed that may figure as the first step towards banishing capital punishment, and the reign of terror, from our land. I have no doubt that such an act of mercy will bring—not more murder, but grace in its train. For when we take away this dark blot from the historic canvas of this country, we do polish that lost pearl, and empower ourselves to gain a first glimpse of the light of the morning sun.

8/14

I am staying in a bed-and-breakfast several miles from the Texas Resource Center in southcentral Houston. Houston, like Los Angeles, is an enormous sprawl. The downtown area that sports one high-rise after another remains relatively confined; beyond its precincts lie mile after mile of what no Chicagoan would call either "city" or "suburb." And yet, surprisingly enough, the general aura of the area is not unpleasant. There is enough nature here, enough tree, grass, and flower, to soften the atmosphere considerably. The place would be quite livable if it weren't for the fierce heat; Texas is in the midst of a gripping drought, and even now, in August, the summer green is tinged with a sere shade of yellow that does not speak of autumnal leavings.

It is early morning; I am sitting in the sunporch of the B&B, enjoying the quiet light here, where it is cool inside, where the sun gives nothing but light. I am thinking about the elements: heat, and light, and the darkness out of which I have just emerged, and to which I will return tonight; I am thinking how little we know about all these things that have been, and will be forever, not merely the condition of existence but, as well, the vocabulary of the spirit. For so soon as we open our mouth to speak of grief and joy, do we not transform into fountains of light and cradles of darkness, crucibles of burning fire, or celebrants of dawn? And should one not hope and pray that all the poetry that has poured forth from our travail—all the religious words that catch and contain our experience of these first things—would have filled our urn with wisdom; that, in the course of centuries, we ourselves would have finally learned to mix darkness and light in the laws of our life, molded our vessels so as to contain their primal changes, so that the kiss of any human mouth would be as a draught of well-aged wine? But history, it seems, has not sufficed to hold very well the shinings of the spirit. Our consciousness is burned and cracked; our land, a plot of parched soil broken into a thousand pieces that cannot bear the Tree of Life.

After breakfast and some reading, I am off to Texas Southern University Law School where "Graham Case Hearings" will take place at noon in the Moot Court Room. This is in no wise an official juridical proceeding, but rather an event organized by the Graham Coalition for the purpose of public (and, of course, press) education. The primary idea is to give LDF/TRC lawyers a chance to present the arguments and (above all) the evidence of Graham's innocence which has not been heard in any federal or state court. Respected figures from the Texas legal and political community will play the role of "the court."

The mood today is more somber than yesterday, for the word from the lawyers, now, is that Gary Graham is not yet by any means home free—not even for the time being, not even with respect to the execution still officially on the books for Monday night. The victory won by Gary Graham in the state court, it turns out, is precarious; the ruling is an unusual one, and there is a question as to whether or not Judge Lowry actually has the jurisdiction to enter the order he handed down. Graham's lawyers are virtually certain that the district attorney's office will appeal the decision to the higher court (the Court of Criminal Appeals) first thing Monday morning, requesting that Lowry's stay be vacated and the execution be allowed to go forward as scheduled.

In such procedural matters, the court can and will act quickly: It will decide the matter, one way or another, on Monday. No one knows how the five-judge court will rule; the lawyers set the odds at about 50-50. If the decision goes the wrong way, Gary Graham will be executed, as scheduled, by the state of Texas just after midnight, August 17, 1994.

So, though this court is "moot," the matter at hand is not, and a sense of dramatic tension pervades the proceedings.

The Graham Case Hearings begin at high noon. As I make my way across the TSU grounds, the sun is at its zenith, and the harsh, bright light casts few shadows. The campus is largely deserted; no summer session competes with the August heat. The law school is situated off by itself in a modern building undistinguished by anything other than the shade offered by its solid walls.

Inside, people are milling in the glassed-in lobby. I find my way to the moot court, a large, shell-shaped room sealed off from the outside. The windowless space is already half-full, and a number of news cameras are swiveling around the periphery. Soon, the "court" is called to order, and the proceedings begin.

Richard Burr of the NAACP Legal Defense Fund (one of Graham's chief attorneys) begins with a basic outline of the systematic faults in the Texas legal system; presenting, essentially, the substance of the federal suit rejected just yesterday. Burr begins by stressing a general theme that recurs, again and again, in dialogue about "*Graham vs. Texas*": namely, that the "jurisdiction" of this case extends far beyond the narrow bounds of one man's individual life; that Graham's situation is a symptom and symbol of forces that act upon many, and in which all are—consciously or not—implicated Burr's more specific message: What we see reflected in the case of Gary Graham is a prime instance of a criminal justice *system in failure*. And, predictably, those whom the system primarily (though not exclusively) *fails* are poor minorities, especially (in this region at least) African Americans. In the domain of criminal (and perhaps especially) capital law, race *and* class matter.

Now, then, Burr outlines some of the points I read about yesterday, arguing that

(1) AFRICAN AMERICANS ARE SO DISPROPORTION-ATELY IMPRISONED AND SENTENCED TO DEATH IN TEXAS THAT THE [federal justice] DEPARTMENT MUST INTERVENE TO PROTECT THE RIGHT OF AFRICAN AMERICANS TO BE FREE OF THE ODIOUS INFLUENCE OF RACIAL BIAS IN THE CRIMINAL JUSTICE SYSTEM.

Numbers begin pouring from the lively lawyer's mouth. "African Americans make up only 12% of the population of Texas, yet are 48% of its prison population; Whites, on the other hand, make up 63% of the general population, yet are only 29% of the prison population. For every 100,000 African Americans in Texas, 1,415 are in prison, but for every 100,000 white people, only 167 are in prison. Thus, the rate at which blacks are incarcerated is nearly nine times that of the rate at which whites are incarcerated."

We hear, too, that racial disparities exist as well in the composition of death row; that— though the disparities here tend to be somewhat less marked than those of the general prison population—in *Harris Country,* the death row disparities roughly *match* the statewide numbers, and (a fact relevant to Gary Graham) are most accentuated for youthful offenders sentenced to death.

Of course—Burr admits—these are "just numbers," and numbers themselves never convince. There is always the common-sense possibility that the disparities reflect, at least in significant part, not racial bias in the criminal justice system, but the higher rate of crime in the black community. Burr notes, too, the relevant legal background:

> "Mr. Graham is cognizant of the legal and factual framework within which the disparities will be viewed. He is aware that the Supreme Court has held in McCleskey v. Kemp, 481 U.S. 279 (1987), that statistical disparities alone cannot establish that racial bias has influenced the criminal justice process . . . ."

But Burr has answers to these doubts: Though it is impossible to attain certainty in the matter, *"raw statistical disparities"* of the kind evident in Texas, when subject to accepted forms of analysis *"almost invariably reveal that racial bias is a significant factor influencing the outcome of criminal proceedings."* Moreover, the statistic disparities are not put forth as *proof* but as *"substantial basis for concern and as a compelling reason—in effect "probable cause"—for an . . . investigation of the influence of racial bias in the criminal justice process in Texas."*

And, of course, "probable cause" for assuming that *if* Gary Graham were white, or (still more importantly), Bobby Lambert were not, Gary Graham might well not be sitting on death row today, his life hanging by thinnest of legal threads.

As I listen, my mind fills in some footnotes. I know, for instance, that the argument that the institution of capital punishment is, in *practice*—if not theory—race- and class-based, can be made not only for Texas, but for most every state of the union that boasts the penalty of death. The Graham Hearings naturally focus on Texas, but some national numbers may be of interest here. At the time of this writing, since the Furman decision resuscitated the death sentence in 1976, there have been 253 individuals executed, 140 Whites (55.33%), 97 Blacks (38.44%), 15 Latinos (5.93%), and 1 Native American (.39%). The breakdown of the 341 *victims* involved reads as follows: 288 whites (84.46%), 40 blacks (11.73%), 8 Latinos (2.35%), 5 Asians (1.46%).

These basic numbers indicate what is, in fact, common knowledge among most all those involved, one way or another, with what may well qualify, today, as America's most peculiar institution: namely that the race of the victim counts as a most significant factor in determining who does and does not receive the sentence of death. Millard Farmer, a lawyer legendary for his death penalty work, states the general rule: "race, poverty, and geography determine who gets the death penalty—if the victim is white, if the defendant is poor and whether or not the local D.A. is willing to plea bargain." Though the two prongs of the devil's pitchfork—selective enforcement and prosecution, and inadequate public defense—may not be so quite so sharp in other states as they are in Texas, they are nonetheless hard at work sending (a disproportionate number of) poor non-White peoples to the hell that is death row.

Burr, in his argument, mentioned the important McCleskey case. Though he did not mention Justice Brennan's dissent in that case, he might well have, for it is surely a most eloquent expression of the argument Burr is putting forth:

> *At some point in his case, Warren McCleskey doubtless asked his lawyer whether a jury was likely to sentence him to die. A candid reply to this question would have been disturbing. First, counsel would have to tell McCleskey that few of the details of*

the crime or of McCleskey's past criminal conduct were more important than the fact that his victim was white. The story could be told in a variety of ways, but McClesky could not fail to grasp its essential narrative line: there was a significant chance that race would play a prominent role in determining if he lived or died.

It is tempting to pretend that minorities on death row share a fate in no way connected to our own, that our treatment of them sounds no echoes beyond the chambers in which they die. Such an illusion is ultimately corrosive, for the reverberations of injustice are not so easily confined. The destinies of the two races in this country are indissolubly linked together, and the way in which we choose those who will die reveals the depth of moral commitment among the living.

The Court's decision today will not change what attorneys in Georgia tell other Warren McCleskeys about their chances of execution. Nothing will soften the harsh message they must convey, nor alter the prospect that race undoubtedly will continue to be a topic of discussion. McCleskey's evidence will not have obtained judicial acceptance, but that will not affect what is said on death row. However many criticisms of today's decision may be rendered, these painful conversations will serve as the most eloquent dissents of all.

Burr is still speaking, arguing, now, his second main point—that Texas state regulation makes it *nigh impossible* for indigent defendants to receive anything like adequate legal counsel. After the blunt statement that "... *One of the most striking features of the Texas system is that the state has assumed no responsibility for it* . . ." Burr ticks off the relevant facts. In most states that permit capital punishment, state funds are set aside for indigent defense in capital cases; Texas does no such thing. As a result, the money available for the court-appointed attorneys that act as counsel in the vast majority of cases is abysmally low. As well, Texas (again, unlike most death penalty states) fails to supply a state-mandated public defender system. This denies support services and backup resources to the private attorneys who shoulder the burden of the defense.

Burr's oration is clear and emphatic; his delivery obviously indebted to the brief he has coauthored, which sums this phase of the case in these words:

> Taken together, the inadequacies of Texas' indigent defense system make it extremely unlikely that any lawyer appointed to a capital case will be able to provide effective assistance. Attorneys likely to be appointed are those who are willing to take cases for which they will be paid no more than $50 per hour—far less than is necessary to sustain a law practice. If they have the requisite training and experience to know how to represent people effectively in death cases, it is sheer coincidence; their appointment is not likely to turn on relevant training and experience. The odds that they will be paid at all . . . for the time they devote to the case out of the court are about 50-50. And if they hire an investigator or expert, the odds of being reimbursed fully or even substantially for the services of the investigator or expert are far less than 50-50. Finally, these attorneys will have no easily accessed source of support and expertise . . .

> . . . In sum, lawyers appointed to capital cases in Texas are likely to be those whose practices are not thriving, who have none of the special expertise necessary for capital defense work, who are encouraged not to work on their clients' cases out of court or to hire others to help do so, and who cannot get the help they need to do a minimally adequate job at repre-

senting their clients . . . The system is stacked . . . toward producing representation that is inadequate . . . .

Burr closes his case. Criminal justice in Texas is a system in failure, and that is our problem. It is not merely, or primarily Gary Graham, but rather "we the people," American citizens, who are on trial.

Trying to process the implications of Burr's presentation, another phrase of Millard Farmer's comes back to me—one that helps me put the issue in perspective. I write it down and end this phase of the case with my own reflections:

"The death penalty is *part of the political process, it is not* part of the criminal justice system." —Millard Farmer

The notion of the law's silver hammer striking cleanly and righteously down upon just those heads who have most violated the social contract is a fiction of the popular imagination. Capital punishment, as a social and institutional fact does not work that way. At the least, one might think, our common sense of justice would demand that the harshest of retributions should be reserved for the worst of crimes, but in fact the heinousness of the crime seldom, if ever, proves the decisive factor. Race, class, and local politics rule.

But the popular imagination inevitably tends to de-historicize the issue, and idealize the sentence of death. Gripped—and understandably so—by the horror and injustice of each individual murder—the angry citizenry demands satisfaction for the egregious wrong. And too many politicians are ready and willing to oblige, unwilling to see and say that to answer one (private) crime against humanity with another (civil) one does not work to confine, but (perforce) merely widens the expanding orbit of violence. When and where will it stop?

After Burr, several other speakers address "the court" and the crowd, including Reverend Boney, who once more takes Burr's "case" right up to the highest court of appeal. Rehearsing particulars of Graham's own case, he (like Burr) emphasizes that capital punishment is a form of institutional racism. He does not, however, speak vindictively, and stresses that the spiritual and social wounds that surface in the institution advertise not moral or spiritual bankruptcy but a need for a true ministry, a real healing. Though Reverend Boney does not want to stray too far from the primarily legal text established by the setting, he lets us know, in no uncertain terms, that the issue of capital punishment is no narrow legal matter, but an ethical and social concern of the highest import; and, in fact, it presents a profound spiritual challenge that cannot and will not be met by those who allow themselves to be ruled by the base emotion of fear and vengeance. He ends with a quotation from another preacher:

"Church is for people who don't want to go to Hell; Religion for those who have been there and back."

But the leading role in this hearing is clearly reserved not for the lawyer or the priest but rather for those individuals in the position to give the most powerful testimony of Graham's actual innocence: either as *eyewitnesses* present at the scene of the crime or *alibi witnesses* testifying to the fact that Graham was elsewhere the night of the crime. There are a total of 11 such witnesses: six eyewitnesses, and five alibi witnesses, all of whom have given testimony indicating Graham's innocence, and quite a few of them are here, today—though not all of them in person.

Another one of Graham's lawyers—TRC lawyer Anthony Houghton—has given us a quick briefing on the status of evidence, stressing that *none* of the testimony we are about to witness has ever been admitted into a court of law on account of the "30-day rule." Gary Graham, Houghton emphasizes, is not begging for mercy, but for justice. And what might "justice" have to say about the matter? First and foremost, *"Let the evidence be heard."* It is a phrase I will soon hear again, resonating in the streets of downtown Houston.

But now another voice and another image occupy my attention. Houghton has finished speaking, wheeled a large video machine into a position where it can be seen by all, and flicked the switch. One of the witnesses is about to share her testimony with us from inside the magic screen.

As the video image comes into focus, we see a middle-aged Black woman; Mrs. Wilma Amos is offering us her account of the night of May 13. She was shopping at Safeway that night and saw both Bobby Lambert and the man who shot him shortly thereafter inside the store—in fact, she saw Lambert's killer on at least *three* separate occasions inside the store. As she left the Safeway to go to her van, she noticed the scuffle between the men she had seen inside; a gun was fired, and the assailant "passed by her at a distance just out of arm's reach about three or four feet and paused and stared at (me) for a second or two and then ran away." Wilma Amos stresses that she was "POSITIVE" that the assailant was not a tall man—that he was about 5'5". She is also certain that Gary Graham was NOT the person she saw first in the store and then in the parking lot; was not the person who killed Bobby Lambert.

On the video, Mrs. Amos' interlocutor finishes the session with a question concerning Graham's initial trial, at which she did testify. (At trial, remember, the general rule is that witnesses supply information in *response* to questions posed by attorneys. If a relevant question is not asked, relevant information may not find voice.) During that trial, was she ever asked whether or not Gary Graham was the suspect she saw at the Safeway? Wilma Amos shakes her head. No. No. No.

After Wilma Amos, we see and hear several other witnesses on the video, all of whom tell variations of the same story. Ronald Hubbard was a Safeway employee who saw Lambert's assailant; he described the suspect as a man of middle height, about 5'5". Hubbard was shown a police lineup that included Gary Graham; he told police he did not see anyone who resembled the killer. Ronald Hubbard was never called to testify. Leodis Wilkerson was 12 years old at the time of the crime and witnessed Lambert's killing. He, too, when interviewed, claimed to be absolutely sure that the assailant was shorter than 5'6" Bobby Lambert himself. Though the prosecutor's file included Wilkerson's name as witness, he—like Hubbard—never testified at trial.

The voices on the video echo through the hushed court; the attention of the entire room is fixed upon the faces on the screen, the expostulations, the expressions. It is difficult to doubt the sincerity of these people; very difficult to imagine that they are not telling the truth; very, very difficult to believe, in view of all these faces, just now fading from the screen, that Gary Graham is a guilty man.

But the testimony here, in this moot court, will not stop at faces on a screen, interviewed by a faceless interlocutor. Just now, Anthony Houghton—stage center once more—is calling to "the stand" another witness. A spare Black man rises from the edge of the audience, somewhat uncertainly "takes the stand," and prepares to give his testimony—in person.

Houghton: Mr. Stevens, does the date May 13, 1981, mean anything in particular to you? Stevens: Yes, sir.

H: Mr. Stevens, can you tell us what that date means to you?

S: I know that is the night Mr. Lambert was shot at the Safeway.

H: How do you know that, Mr. Stevens?

S: Because I was there that night, when it happened.

H: Where exactly were you, that night, Mr. Stevens, when the crime took place? Did you witness the crime?

S: No, sir, I didn't see the murder happen, but as I was driving into the Safeway that night—my wife was with me in the car— we saw a young Black guy running out of the lot. He ran right in front of our car as we were coming in—I had to put on the brakes so as not to hit him. Then he ran on out.

H: Did you see anything else after that?

S: Yes, sir. I saw somebody—Mr. Lambert—kind of staggering toward the store, as if he'd been shot.

H: Did you get a good look at the man who ran in front of your car that night?

S: Yes, sir.

H: How? You said he was running.

S: Yes, sir, he was. But he stopped for a second when I almost hit him—when I put on the brakes—and looked right at us for a moment. Then he ran on out of the lot.

H: How would you describe this man? What did he look like?

S: He was a young Black guy, about 5'5", compact, not big, with short hair, and no beard or anything like that.

H: Mr. Stevens, do you know what Gary Graham looks like?

S: Yes, sir.

H: Tell us how you know what Mr. Graham looks like, and, on that basis, whether or not you think he could have been the man that ran in front of your car that night.

S: Well, I've seen pictures of him, and then, this April, I saw two stories about Gary Graham's case on television . . . one on Channel 11 and one on "City Under Siege." Both stories had Gary Graham on them. They had him on videotape from the prison where he is now, and they had pictures of how he looked back in 1981, when the murder took place. When I saw these pictures, I knew that Gary Graham was not the person I saw run in front of my car at the Safeway parking lot the night the man was shot there. I am sure of that. They have the wrong person for this murder.

H: Mr. Stevens, you've seen Gary Graham recently on television, but how fresh is your memory of the man who ran in front of your car at this point? It's been a long time, and you saw him for such a short time.

S: Yes, but I saw him again afterwards, and that refreshed my memory.

H: Saw him again, Mr. Stevens? When? Please detail the circumstances.

S: A little over a year after the murder, sometime in 1982, I ran into the guy who I saw in front of my car that night at the Safeway. I met him several times more after that, in 1983 and in 1985. I first met him at an apartment complex near Little York and Northline. I talked with him for about five minutes. He seemed to be somebody I knew, but I couldn't place him at first. After I learned more about him, I put it together: He was the guy that ran in front of my car at the Safeway the night of the murder.

This guy looked just the same as he did that night at the Safeway. He was a young Black man, with brown skin, short hair, and no facial hair. He was well built, about 160-pounds, and short, about 5'3 or 5'4". He had a mean look in his face, but he did not sound mean when he talked.

H: Mr. Stevens, one last—two last questions. Were you ever shown the composite sketch of the assailants which Bernadine Skillern helped police artists put together after the crime?

S: Yes, sir, I was shown this picture earlier this year.

H: What can you say about that sketch? In your opinion, did it look like the man you saw run in front of your car or Gary Graham?

S: After seeing the sketch, I can say that is how the person looked who ran in front of my car—the same guy that I saw several times during 1982, 1983, and 1985. Gary Graham does not look anything like this guy.

H: That will be all. Thank you, Mr. Stevens, thank you very much.

All the witnesses I've told you about so far are eyewitnesses; persons present at the scene of the crime. I have not detailed the evidence of the five alibi witnesses—Loraine Johnson, William Chambers, Dorothy Shields, Mary Brown, and Vanessa Ford. These people are all relatives or friends of Graham, a fact that naturally induces some skepticism. But of course it is unreasonable to assume that relatives are incapable of telling the truth—especially when so many stories, with so many details, match so closely. We had already heard one of these witnesses – William Chambers—on the video, but after Mr. Stevens' testimony, another— Loraine Johnson—rises and gives voice to the basic facts affirmed by all the alibi witnesses: The night that Bobby Lambert was killed, Gary Graham was taking part in a family barbecue, 15 miles away from the scene of the crime.

The Graham hearings draw to a close. Feet shuffle, briefcases are closed. I rise, stiffly, and exit the dim, confining room.

Outside, the fierce sun shines.

That evening, ensconced in my comfortable room in the B&B, inside the cocoon of dark green curtains, wooden dressers, and a large double bed I do not need, I am reading; reading and thinking back on the day's events.

After the moot court at TSU, I had visited another, better-known school, in part to see if I couldn't locate a colleague from Cornell who I knew had secured a job at Rice a few years before. He, too, was an Emerson scholar, and I was thinking it would be interesting to share with him some of what I was experiencing and perhaps discuss the cultural and intellectual ramifications of capital punishment. The issue is one that should, *theoretically,* grab the attention of the academy. What, after all, could be more relevant to the academy's current concerns than resistance to a racist, classist institution readily seen as a vestige of slavery; what more "politically correct" than abolition?

Rice University is spacious; the buildings and grounds characterized by that distinctive self-possessed grandeur that one finds in European palaces and (in a somewhat different guise) the Southern plantation—that peculiar quality of genteel propriety that imparts an almost classical aura to the fact of ownership, extending this out over a whole landscape or even country not in the admiring manner of the artist but rather after the fashion of that form of mastery, that style of life that tends to *give* rather than *take* commands even to nature or (what for Cole and Emerson would be the same thing) God. And so after what was already a long walk on the crushed gravel paths that led through the catalpa trees and across the lawns you pass through the arched opening in the line of white buildings imposing almost as a fort and walk again across a spacious lawn towards a fountain and then white columns, the white columns of a building that in imagination if not in fact could once have been owned by nobility or landed gentry but now is an estate of quite another order, another unreal city, from there to move through the double glass doors and mazy halls to ask the proper well-attired person of whatever color behind the desk in whatever offices houses whatever department one is supposedly "in" for the address of a friend, for a human connection to the soul of the past, for a living connection to the history one is living and receives only mute, uncomprehending stares before at last being turned away because such a person is no longer there and so in fact no longer exists for them and you remember once again that this isn't it, that you've come to the wrong place. And so as usual you find the room where they keep the books, the place where you can open doors and still hear voices real human voices no matter how distant or dim or dead no matter how many times the aloneness, the deep aloneness that assails you at night drives you to them as to what very well could be your grave as if you were some crazy 16-year-old white boy digging up a Gowrie in the church on Beat Four just to save some insolent Negro's (and you don't even know if he did it) ass. And then finally though you're still in the middle and don't know what happens you've read enough to forget there is no need for the large double bed though now you remember you wish to God there were and so the book doesn't go on the wooden table but stays there where a warm body or rather a face might be but isn't by your pillow and the dark green curtains are looking even darker in the dim light as you reach up for the light cord that you wish sometimes could put it all out just like that but then there's always the blistering aftershock of another day, another life because even *they* can't put out the sun and then you are tossing and turning for what could be hours there in the dark and then it hits you there in the dark that maybe this is it, maybe this is why you're here.

8/15

Sunday morning; another cloudless day. Light streams through the green curtains; ghosts dance on the carpet. Rising out of the dim realm that belongs neither to the dead nor to the living, that border state between sleep and wakefulness I hear:

> A voice that cries, "The tomb in Palestine
> Is not the voice of spirits lingering.
> It is the grave of Jesus, where he lay."
> We live in an old chaos of the sun,
> Or old dependency of day and night . . .

. . . and, after ablutions, stumble into breakfast, where faces as round as cereal bowls and the silverware shines.

Later today, in downtown Houston, there will be a march and rally for Gary Graham. Shy of crowds and loudspeakers, I will nonetheless be there, just as I will be one of the relatively few white faces amidst the sea of black in the huge hall in the belly of the Hyatt Regency listening to the leader of the Nation of Islam speak on behalf of Gary Graham tonight, when the march and rally end.

For now, however, I am in desperate need of another sort of historical and cultural relief, and—after breakfast and some desultory reading—am on my way to visit an art museum—the Menil Collection and the adjacent Rothko Chapel, a sanctuary specially designed to house paintings of the renowned Abstract Expressionist.

The chapel and the museum both owe their existence to John and Dominique de Menil. "French, cultivated, cosmopolitan"—and extraordinarily wealthy on account of Dominique's family's petroleum-related industry—the de Menils moved from Paris to Houston in the upheaval of World War II. There Dominique de Menil, having converted to Roman Catholicism, began collecting art under the tutelage of Father Marie-Alain Couturier, "a Dominican priest and painter active in a then controversial movement to revive sacred art by involving living artists—modern, advanced, secular ones—in the decoration of Catholic churches." By 1985, the de Menils had collected 10,000 objects, concentrating on African tribal items, Mediterranean antiquities, and modern European and American art.

Dominique de Menil: "When you stop buying, you are history."

In the 1960s, the de Menils funded the creation of the Rothko chapel, a combination of art and architecture that recalls, in some wise, the Matisse chapel in Vence. Finally, in 1987, Dominique de Menil supplied an appropriate environment for her own extensive collection, building this well-appointed private museum one block from the now renowned Rothko Chapel.

There are many beautiful things in the Menil Collection. I am specially drawn to *Dove Flying*, a small, sixth-century stone figurine from Greece and (part of a special exhibition) certain French tapestries that offer colorful allegories of virtue, courage, love.

Yet despite the quality of the collection, I have trouble focusing. The stress and strangeness of the last few days have exhausted me. Staring at the centuries-old weave of the tapestry fabric, lids heavy with the weight of lost nights shutter my eyes. The de Menils may have managed the transition from Paris to Texas with singular aplomb, but *I* am no King of the Road today and feel rather like the sorry sequel of a former self; like a mind, a life, an eye that has lost its wide-angled lens and the reassuring click of the camera, that is no longer the projector of magic light that makes the figures play, but is rather one more wanderer lost in a hall of mirrors, a nomad adrift in some vast and historic desert so that this museum and this tapestry appear to me a kind of mirage, an oasis that holds no water—for here there is no water, no Mediterranean Sea, no Rhone River or rain or even sluggish Seine to temper the constant heat of the sun; nor does manufactured cool refresh the pilgrim on his way. The voice of my guide has disappeared in the late summer's swirling dust, or rather—intruded into regions that leave me dizzily wondering where I am, feeling adrift even though I still see signs showing and telling where I am amongst these scenes and sights that *should* be more familiar and yet appear to me more strange than anything I saw abroad, for *there* history if not kind or good still exhibited an organized and legible if exhausted order, and though all was written in a foreign language I could still sometimes try to translate, and still sometimes even almost understand; but here in the depths of Texas, the Cluny and the Louvre seem part of a distant dream from which I have not exactly awakened but am no longer really in— as if I were in the midst of transition, as if dwelling in that time or place *between* when the reels of the world are being rewound; and the strange parapsychological association between the case (or face) of Gary Graham and the textile *Lady and the Unicorn*, the coincidence of which was the *p'oint d'appui* of this voyage remains as much or more of a mystery to me as ever here, now, almost three months later; after traveling to Paris to see The Lady face to face, after coming to Houston, where I myself am a mote in the dust storm that swirls around the figure of the caged Black man condemned without justice to die.

Not that there have *not* been further associations, not that there have not been more of those twinings of life and thought that weave *our* tapestries— the texts that bear, within their subtle, intricate, and infinitely variegated designs not so much the *law* of those truths by which a person, a nation, a world might live, but rather those *signs* in and through which the Book of Life may be read as well as written; those virtually invisible nigh indiscernible indications that stem from a soil not burned into the unyielding crust that breaks the mouths of those who seek to assuage their hunger, fear, and rage with the hardnesses it bears, but rather the still rich and fertile soil pregnant with the seeds of things that do not so much *predict* as *intimate* a future, indemnifying it (so far as is possible) against the past, clearing the way for a new world that would be part of history perhaps and yet at the same time *beyond* all that has ever been covered by that term, a momentary interregnum that would finally be not so much the end of human time as its recommencement, a genesis occurring in the midst of history itself, born of its, of our travail, out of the womb of the undesecrated death of races and of nations.

... *The intellectual would of course have to be from the start an opponent and disavower of revolutions; he of all people knows how slowly all changes of lasting significance are accomplished, how inconspicuous they are and, through their very slowness, almost imperceptible, and how Nature, in her constructive zeal, hardly anywhere lets intellectual forces come to the fore. And yet on the other hand it is the same intellectual who, by reason of his insight, grows impatient when he sees in what miscarried and muddled conditions human things are content and persist: indeed, we are all continually experiencing the fact that this and that—almost everything—needs changing (and that at the root): life, this infinitely rich, infinitely generous life, that is permitted to be cruel only by very reason of its inexhaustibility: life itself—in how many instances it simply cannot make itself effective any more, pushed aside as it is by a lot of secondary institutions, grown lazy by their continuance—who would not often wish for a great storm that would tear down everything obstructive and infirm, to make room for the again creative infinitely young, infinitely benevolent forces.*

. . . Strictly speaking, the unswerving intellectual could side with neither party in this chaotically confused struggle which the poison of the stagnated war—turned back as it was into the country—further and further provoked; neither with those who drove ruthlessly ahead nor with those who met the often criminal outbreaks of this insanity with old and no less unjust and inhuman means: the future lay with neither, and to it the intellectual is after all allied and sworn, not in the sense of the revolutionary, who would presume to create from one day to the next a humanity freed (what is freedom?) and happy (what is happiness?), but in that other patient understanding that he is preparing in people's hearts those subtle, secret, tremulous transformations out of which alone will proceed the agreements and unities of a more clarified future.

—Rilke, letter to Countess Aline Dietrichstein
August 6, 1919, Soglio, Switzerland

I do not know exactly what it was that recalled Rilke to mind; probably nothing more than the fact of the tapestry itself, the French characters, the thread of color running through the summer months as if in some kind of anxious prolepsis of a fall that would, this time, be different; a fall that would not be a plunge *away* from love and grace, but *toward* it; a descent, a leaving, a departure not from the privilege of a *Paradise* that never can exist but from the historical *Hell* that always has; enabling, finally, the acceptance of a mode of Being that is and always will be the true human estate not in the form of eternity perhaps but enduring rather in the rhythm of perpetual renewal born out of the polar flux of the invisible heartfelt transitions and elemental longings of our kind.

I have no time for the quiet refuge of Rothko Chapel. I will return to visit that tomorrow. For now, I must go back to my room for some rest—some sleep to see me through the rest of the long nightlike day.

~

Justice Now! Let the evidence be heard! Justice Now! Let the Evidence be heard! Justice Now! Let the Evidence ...

I am in the midst of the march; one in a long two-by-two column of people moving through the steely city, issuing a chant reverberating along the high-rise-lined streets of downtown Houston early this August evening. Reverend Bony, equipped with bullhorn and walking staff, leads; he and a few others keep the double file of a hundred or more faces more or less in step as it snakes from the Family Law Center to the federal courthouse chanting:

Justice Now! Let the Evidence be Heard! Justice Now! Let the evidence be heard! Justice Now! Let the Evidence be Heard!

... while the few bystanders or passers-by (it is a sultry Sunday evening and the streets are quiet) watch and sometimes even wave.

And now the undulating line of marchers, complete with police escort, nears and halts by the entrance of the courthouse where a variety of speakers upbraid the system thank someone for their support exhort commitment to the cause, while around the periphery of the sometimes sober, sometimes cheering crowd blue-uniformed police officers look indifferently on.

Less than an hour after the first step, the final speaker finishes, and the crowd disperses. Many, however, go in the same direction, walking—as I am walking—through lines of Houston high-rises to the Hyatt Regency to hear the leader of the Nation of Islam speak on behalf of Gary Graham—or rather, on behalf of the justice of his cause.

～

There must be several thousand people sitting on the small metal folding chairs in the huge hall in the Hyatt; the atmosphere is filled with expectation. The formal order of the Black Muslim organization is a just discernable background of the scene, represented by the handful of distinctively attired "ushers" standing by columns or moving round the periphery. But the general sense of gathered and more or less naturally relaxed humanity absorbs even these official stances and masked visages readily enough; when I ask after the water reserved for some official reception on the single long table in the back of the room, I am cordially told to help myself by a face that can move and even smile. The elements hold: Everyone around here understands the sometimes terrible need for water.

A few preliminaries precede the evening's main event. Several speakers (including Minister Robert Muhammad) step to the podium on the raised stage to say a few words; are greeted, and sent off with applause. And now the master of ceremonies is informing us of something else that all are too prone to forget, but which must be attended to. An energetic young man obviously suited to the part climbs onstage and begins calling upon the people to contribute to Gary Graham's legal and political defense:

"One Hundred Dollars—One Hundred Dollars—who is going to start us off with the first One Hundred Dollars . . ."

and—just as a deep current pushing against a snag will at last cut loose, turn, and (for a moment) *lift* a single dark brown log out of the deep river breaking the jam—so eventually, inevitably, the mounting tension in the hall forces the first long, dark arm up out of the midst of the people, and the ringing voice calls the victory out loud and clear and then it is off and running: hands waving hats passing and the mobile ushers going up front and calling out the names of the givers of 100, of 50, of 25 dollars:

"Brother Calvin, *Brother* James, *Sister* Newson . . ."

until, perhaps, the collective will merges momentarily with the unalterable necessity of communal defense against the nameless force that would submerge and drown all Brothers and Sisters and all personal names, keeping them (us) down for good if it could, if given half the chance.

~

The first words out of Minister Louis Farrakhan's mouth are a plea— directed, particularly, to the press—for a fair hearing; an appeal to them to listen, objectively, to the man they hear *tonight* and the words he speaks *in this room.* Louis Farrakhan is a most controversial figure, but as I am here, tonight, as a friend of Graham's cause, I seek to honor his appeal.

I would like to report the talk verbatim but cannot. I can only offer my own creative rendition of Farrakhan's speech, drafted from my notes and phrased—to the best of my limited abilities—to capture as accurately as possible the rhetorical energy as well as the sense of the minister's oration.

In times of trial, it is incumbent upon us to study the Creator, and so seek to understand the way in which He rules. For when a society suffers from endemic wrong, and the weight of evil lies heavy on the scale of social justice, then God sends a judgment down to preserve his law among us.

We must strive, then, to view the case of Gary Graham in a religious as well as historical light; must seek to see the significance of the event within the context of our vision of the Creator, and the terms of his eternal rule. It is exactly the grave portent of this case that drives us to the extremity of religious insight, for we know that if justice is done by those in power, God need not correct our judgment with his own. It is only when the law of man falls away from that of God that judgment will come to set it right.

Nor can we, as mortal human beings, predict the time and season of the judgments of the Creator, and should not be careless or hasty in our reading of his ways. Justice delayed is not justice denied, for it is the will of God to allow us the freedom to choose our course. We can accept his guidance, and act in accordance with justice and true law, in which case we will be rewarded by the grace of his spirit; or we can go our own way, refusing the manifest guidance of God's great will. In this case, too, we will inevitably reap our "reward" and meet the consequences of our act.

In the present instance, the choice is clear. It is incumbent upon society to rectify the travesty of justice by allowing the evidence of Gary Graham's innocence to be heard in the court. Anything less makes a mockery of law.

But historical man is too often poor in heart and mind. He does injustice, and when a messenger comes bearing the truth of the judgment thus incurred, he still does not like to mend his wrong, but compounds his error by despising and rejecting God's messengers. But still God is merciful and does not doom his reprobate children, for still he wishes to grant us time to correct our ways, and embrace the love and justice of the true, the God-given law.

And so there is implied in the words of all who bring the news of God an urgent summons that is at once a warning and threat. And let it be understood that it is not the person of the messenger that is from the essence of God, but rather the character of the message which commands our hearing. And so does every prophet say: Do not look upon me, but rather to the law I bear; not upon my face, but to the invisible prospect of my God. This is the way of our religious tradition, in the Bible as well as the Koran. And the jurisprudence of the West is itself built upon this foundation, is made in the image of God's law as this is delivered in the text of religious scripture.

And yet today, all that establishes and extends the law is broken or is breaking down. The law does not live in the home, the school, the church, in the political arena, or in the country's courts of law. Religious leaders are out of touch with the times, and the corruption of politics has forfeited the respect of the people, who no longer respect the organs of power. The symptoms of social decline are not difficult to perceive. The incidence of violent crime is, perhaps, the clearest warning, and the age of criminal offenders grows younger every year. This terrible violence edges us toward the extremes of change: rebellion, anarchy, revolution.

At the very root of this social deterioration is the plight of the Black people in America. America has jailed Black people in general, and continues to refuse to offer sufficient help to those whose troubles still stem, in large part, from the social violence that brought this people to this land. But let it be remembered that God does not fail to see that the people of his choice endure; that the people who choose Him and his law reap their reward; for only thus does justice live among us.

Let us look now at the present case, and the punishment—the penalty of death—that this society intends to inflict upon the person of Gary Graham. It is true that there is biblical precedent for the practice of capital punishment, but the form and circumstances of its administration in biblical culture bears little resemblance to its American institution. In the time of the Old Testament, a capital offender would not be strapped to an electric chair in some secret chamber, or injected with a poison where no one could see: he or she would suffer death by stoning. Thus the community itself actually administered the death: the whole society took upon itself responsibility for capital punishment of the offender. It was the integrity of society itself that lent this arrangement its authority: each individual was responsible to the whole of the community, and vice versa. The criminal who violated that social contract threatened, by his act, the integral fabric of human being, and so the society, acting as individuals and as a whole, tore him or her out of the texture of life itself. Whatever one may think of the arrangement, it exhibited a certain rigorous consistency, a moral fit between principle and praxis.

But our contemporary situation is quite different. We cannot begin to speak, in this country, of one or two or two thousand criminals who offend against the laws of society, for today American society itself has become savage in heart and mind. The stone in the hand is not the age-old implement of justice, but the desperate and angry fling of citizens in the midst of a society gone mad. Is it not evident that those who cry so loud for retribution do so because the system is not working—because it is broken down, and the social fabric is in shreds?

But why is it so? Has this society lived up to the social contract that alone gives it the right to condemn—and perhaps to kill—the criminal as an aberrant, or must it rather see the criminal as a mirror image of its own historic failure to meet its spiritual obligation to its kind?

We should remember the history of this nation. America was founded by pilgrims fleeing religious persecution in Europe. They were, for the most part, peaceably invited to share this continent by its native people. But how well did they keep the peace treaties they signed? And it was not only the Red man and woman that suffered. This state of Texas itself, and much of the southwest, was forcibly taken from the Mexican people. And then, later, Black people were torn from their native Africa and suffered a social wrong second in the lists of wrong only to total genocide. They were enslaved.

Everyone knows this history—in the abstract. Yet how many take into serious enough account the social cost, the ripple effect spreading out from all the stones taken from the hard ground and hurled at innocent Black men and women throughout time? We are speaking here—not of a private offense of one person against another—but of organized crime committed against a whole people. And the abduction and physical bondage was not the whole of it: You will remember, for instance, that in most cases slaves were not allowed to marry. It was not only the bodies of the black people that were enslaved and subjugated, but the very heart of their human spirit that was subjected to assault.

The ban against marriage was a ban against trust and love of their own kind, deliberately intended to hobble the Black person's emotional development, and cripple her capacity to resist the wrongs visited upon her body and person.

The effects of such social crimes are not signed away with emancipation proclamations. The Black community is still fighting the effects of its physical and spiritual bondage. America has so far failed to properly compensate the Black people for the terrible crime committed against them. And the fact that Black leaders, when they have emerged, have regularly been assassinated immeasurably worsens the historic situation.

I am not saying that the Black people need or want handouts: That is not the kind of help, not the kind compensation to which I am refer-ring. In fact, the first species of necessary, of essential "compensation" is not really "compensation" at all, but merely the extension of basic human rights and liberties due to all people as human beings and as members of a civil society. Before we can even speak of "compensation" for past crimes against the Black race, it is necessary to ensure, insofar as that is possible, that such crimes are not still being committed. This is the first and primary task of the American nation with respect to the Black (or any other historically oppressed) people.

Thus, the first responsibility of the government of the United States is to see to the justice of the laws and institutions administered by it and which represent the organs of its power. No government can absolutely preclude the persistent incidence of racism amongst its citizens; it can, however, seek to eradicate the legacy of slavery from its public laws and institutions.

But what rational citizen, reviewing the facts of the case, can refuse to see that the institution of capital punishment in this country represents a pattern of action essentially continuous with the whole history of the slavery; that the killing of Gary Graham by the United States government would, in fact, be a legal lynching in which the entire body politic would be implicated, a crime against humanity of a piece with all those historically committed against the Black people? And so we ask: What moral right does the government of this nation possess to kill criminal offenders when the institutional organ of this so-called "justice" is steeped in a history of crime far more vicious and far-reaching than that of the most depraved private murderer? And under such circumstance, what God fearing citizen could witness—let alone advocate—the execution of this almost certainly innocent Black man without believing that, sometime, somehow, this nation—already steeped in the blood of its Black brethren—will have to pay a terrible price for its immoral and self-willed ways?

Some may have thought that I came here tonight to threaten retribution in case Gary Graham were executed by the State of Texas tomorrow. I have heard murmurings that, if that were to occur, what could happen afterward might well make Los Angeles look like a campfire. But put your matchsticks back in your pocket. What is that cigarette lighter next to the thunder and lightning of God? It is not the Black man or woman that the citizen and judge has to fear—but his God; not fire or water that will destroy him, but the terrible power of good and of evil vested in his own moral choice. So, choose your way, but do it carefully: Choose in knowledge that God's Will will be done; that, if "sent for," judgment will surely come, and that justice, in time, will reign.

When the children of Israel were mistreated, their prophet finally had to say "let my people go." I need not remind you what happened when Pharaoh didn't listen.

It is said that "as a man thinketh, so is he." If a people are grown cold and heartless, their children act in the manner of the parent's thought. It is also said that one can tell a tree by its fruit. If the American people mistreat their Black brethren and fail to care enough about them even to try to share with them the profits as well as the burdens of their civilization, the nation will surely decay, and the Tree of Life that bears its crown will fall upon the hard and unyielding ground of this-once fertile and God-blessed Land.

After the words, the clapping of hands—thousands of them—
sound like thunder in the night, before fading into restless silence. I
follow a dark flood out of the hall, down hotel corridors, and out into
the strange and dim-lit city.

In my room once more, I read from Rilke's *Book of Hours*:

> *I read it in your Word,*
> *culled it from the history of your gestures*
> *as you cupped the growing world*
> *in the warm hands wise*
> *in circumscription.*
>
> *You said Life out loud and Death*
> *softly, and again and again you said:*
>
> > *Be.*
>
> *But before the first death came*
> *Murder.*
>
> *Then your perfect circle tore,*
> *and a cry came out,*
> *tearing the cloth of voices*
> *that had gathered around you*
> *to speak of you,*
> *to carry you*
> *—bridge of all*
> *abysses.*
>
> *And what they have stammered since*
> *are fragments*
> *of your ancient name.*

8/16

The focus of every pilgrimage journey is the shrine.
—David Freedberg, *The Power of Images*

Visiting the Rothko Chapel today, you have to get yourself to Houston, take a ten-minute cab ride from downtown to the Montrose district, get out at Montrose Boulevard and Branard Street, turn west, cross the small campus of St. Thomas University, enter a quiet neighborhood of modest one- and two-story clapboard or brick homes (all strangely painted a warm, brownish gray), arrive at the intersection of Branard and Yupon, swing around a high bamboo hedge, and walk past the reflecting pool upon which Barnett Newman's 26'-high steel sculpture, Broken Obelisk, has been placed. You are now facing a low, pale—red brick wall, the facade of the Rothko Chapel. You see no steps, no portico, no columns, no crucifixes, no statuary, no spire, no dome, no stained glass, no windows—just a low, simple entrance with two black, wood doors. Plain, cheerless, geometric, with an interior sealed off from the pleasant neighborhood and park outside, the building looks more like a tomb than a chapel . . .

. . . and the colors of the paintings inside match the mood. The 14 enormous, rectangular panels are either pitch black or a maroon so deep it is just a few shades away. Thin margins of slightly lighter tones—perfectly straight, like Newman zips at the border—keep the central color contained, so it doesn't spill over the edge, so it fills rather than moves out of the space of the painting. No diffuse color fields, no luminescent yellows or oranges, but a precise geometry of darkness, intense and unrelieved . . .

Rothko Chapel Interior
(photo by Hickey-Robertson)

Meditating in the center of this Zenlike sanctuary (there is nothing here but four spare wooden benches so absorbed in their own form they do not invite sitting), I feel myself inside the dark shutter of Mind at the edge. The place is peaceful; the dark tomb-womb not dangerous, not threatening; this blackness not the absence of good qualities, but rather the surcease of confusion; not the negation of light, but its hibernal implosion; not the Luciferic fall of space, but the low and secure ceiling of divine qualification, of Marian mood.

And then I *see*—this is the space, the shape, the color of . . .

Death.

Death.

Freed from mis—
representation. *Not* the negation of life, *not*
something that stands at the
end, the definitive, the
final *arrest* but a
space of being
always there: underneath, inside, or all
around—the constant shroud of life's endless
shenanigans that, like the thick black cloth the photographer throws
over his head, allows the stilling of the action, the making and the
recording of the image, the opening of the space of recollection, of
remembrance that connects past and future in a timeless rhythm that
is *not* the perverse and centrifugal force of history's man-made motion
but rather its specific resistance and salvific opposite, the centripetal
in-breathing of the cosmos that gives life pregnant rest, and love a place
to dwell . . . .

> *My life*
> *is not this hurried hour*
> *in which you see me rushing.*
> *I am a Tree*
> *risen against the Background, just one*
> *of my many mouths, the one*
> *that is soonest closed.*
>
> *I am the Rest between two notes*
> *that cannot come*
> *together*
> *because Death interposes its deeper tone.*
>
> *Yet in that dark interval the shivering pitches*
> *blend—*
>
>   *and the Song is saved.*

Broken Obelisk
(photo by Hickey-Robertson)

Stepping out of the meditative and motherly space of the Chapel, one is met by the virile and exalting monument: an obelisk, its tip resting on the tip of a pyramid, surges toward the sky . . . .

Outside, the light shines. Outside, I am looking into the reflecting pool surrounding the Broken Obelisk. I am glad I came here; the place is peaceful, restorative, inspiring me to think and reflect.

Yesterday, amongst all the objects in the museum, I became depressed by the thought that I could find very little of real spiritual value and use *to me* that was specifically American, that bore the mark of my native land: objects, forms, colors, places in which my spirit could dwell and be nourished like a child at its mother's breast. Mostly, this does not bother me: If I am a citizen, I am, first of all, a citizen of the world, equally enfranchised in Arles and New Orleans. History itself is a quilt of ocean crossings, and the path of beauty a sunlike ray of endless migration.

And yet, native place is far from nothing, and I cannot deny a special relation to the sprawling canvas of this country, this vast land I traversed even as a 3-year-old child asleep in the back of a van rolling West on 80, *en route* to the Rockies or Grand Tetons, to Jackson or to Silver Lake. I do not like to think that, after wandering the Old World, that I could not find an open road back home, could never return—a prodigal enriched by his travels—to a house that might take me in, a soil that would acknowledge me as its own, would receive and hold the taproot of my mind in its dark embrace.

But when I look over the geography of my country, I seem to see a land laid waste, a field of fire where the spirit can find no shelter, no food, no rest. No Chartres holds the mystery of centuries safe in the stained glass windows of the walls; no medieval paper mill prints sonnets on the Sorgue; no tapestry delivers a silent sermon in its intricately woven allegory of love. Mountains and rivers without end are not enough to hold me here, for the spirit needs its own special vale in which to build its house, some unique *Vaucluse* that veils us, that supplies the culture of elements which lets love grow and prosper amidst the tangled scenes of nature, and where in this vast land could I build a house or tower, secure in the shade of wise ancestors, prepared for the guidance of a master I might follow with willing if unsure steps?

The one who leads me now—leads me even unto the others that speak to me—never came here and scorned the facile transience of this land, the consumptive habits that spits up time in an unending flood of uprooted things. Yet still I yearn for the weather-beaten boards of my own pioneer cabin; long straight timberlines that might hold memories of my American past in the whirled grain. For a time I haunted the New England town that bred this nation's best Speaker of the House and still recall with what emotion I first saw his hat hanging on a nail in the wall of his Concord home; it seemed to me, then, that the plain piece of felt might well hold all the poet's sermons in its modest bowl and that if I could take it down and wear it, I would speak in tongues; but Emerson's hat still hangs on the nail, no longer expecting the man or woman friend who might call it out to true conversation. There are no more seminars in the Transcendentalist study, and the bottomless pond in the neighboring wood—beset by scores of bathers—no longer reflect the eyes of a man who could think alone.

But here, in the blue water below the broken obelisk, I find a revised image of an aspiring American Self, one still bold enough to mime Zeus' zipper and open the silver lining of a new world; a model of the human spirit soaring to steal creative fire and then—thunderstruck—coming to know the ruin, the tear, the jaggedly irrevocable impossibility of perfection which it (pointed *down* now, like a returning rocket, like a broken pencil) translates to triangular base, to meeting ground, to the face in the reflecting pool that receives this abstract expression of American tragedy into its deepest, bluest eye.

～

Throughout history, monuments have been built where art and religion commingle, where art leads the mind from the visible to the invisible. The caves of Ajanta, Hagia Sophia, the mosques of Damascus and Cordoba, the cathedral of Chartres—to name only a few prestigious ones—are such places. Sumptuous or humble, these sacred monuments awaken the body and engage the soul. They are an invitation to selfless departures, to searching itineraries. They call for hope—hope in the advent of a renewed humankind. A delight to the eyes, they are also a locus for the heart, a habitat of intangibles. Like the shells children place to their ears to listen to the sound of the sea, they induce the sound of a soundless ocean. Many have heard this sound at the Rothko chapel.

—Dominique de Menil

I am seated on a bench near the *Broken Obelisk*, reading the Rothko Chapel's brochure. Not merely a place for private meditation, the Rothko chapel is a place where art, religion, and human rights intersect under the umbrella—not of any one established religion — but of a thoroughly catholic culture of the human spirit. The unique art and architecture defines this universal spiritual character:

The Rothko Chapel . . . is not committed to any one religion; it imposes no particular traditional environment. The chapel is a place of worship receptive to the essence and rites of ceremonies being performed. In recent years, those "ceremonies" have included observances of Puja, Rosh Hashana, Palm Sunday, Good Friday, Eid el-Fitr, Eid el-Adha, Cinco de Mayo Mass, and Now Ruz; Whirling Dervishes from Konya, Turkey presenting Sufi ceremony inside and in front of the Chapel; a prayer for world peace led by His Holiness the Dalai Lama, rituals led by the Gyuto Tantric Monks, the performance of the "Mass for Pentecost Sunday," a work commissioned to commemorate the opening of the Menil Collection . . .

. . . and more. But the charter of the chapel does not stop at art and religion: the dedication of the sculpture by which I am sitting to the Revered Martin Luther King Jr. announces, too, that this is a site dedicated to the cause of human rights:

Since December 10, 1973 the Rothko Chapel has observed the annual celebration of the "Universal Declaration of Human Rights" by the United Nations; in 1981 it established the Awards for Commitment to Truth and Freedom; in 1986 two more important human rights awards were established, the Carter-Menil Human Rights Prize and

The Rothko Chapel Oscar Romero Award—this latter presented that same year by Archbishop Desmond Tutu of South Africa to Bishop Proano of Ecuador. In 1988 the Rothko Chapel organized "Perceptions of Human Rights Issues by Young Americans," a workshop led by students from six Texas universities; in August, 1989, to recognize the bicentennial of the French "Declaration of the Rights of Man and the Citizen," four students who participated in the drafting of the "1989 youth Declaration of Human Rights," in Strasbourg presented this new declaration to U.S. citizens at the Rothko Chapel; in December, 1991, the Chapel celebrated its 20th anniversary by a joint human rights awards ceremony with the Carter Menil Human Rights Foundation. Central America was the focus; the keynote speaker, Nelson Mandela, was given a Special Rothko Chapel award.

I am moved by all this spiritual geography: the fusion of art, religion, politics; the impressive written record. And yet—in light of the circumstances that have brought me here—I cannot read the litany of human rights awards without a sense of deeply disconcerting irony. I did not, after all, come to Houston in order to see the Rothko Chapel. Rather, what brought me here was Houston's own patented human rights horror, the unparalleled efficiency of state-sanctioned killing here that motivated the NCADP (National Committee for the Abolition of the Death Penalty) to advertise its special "Mess with Texas" campaign with a slogan borrowed from the tourist industry: *"Texas: it's like another country."*

It is, to be sure, inspiring to read of the heroic individuals from Latin America or South Africa who have been honored for their efforts here, but to me, now—as I rise from the bench by the *Broken Obelisk* to go back to the TRC offices where, after agonizing hours, I will finally learn whether or not Gary Graham will die tonight—it must inevitably seem that the Rothko Chapel Foundation has left some vital and pressing *homework* undone. By now there is a new South Africa, and Nelson Mandela has made clear that there is no room for the death penalty in a country that has turned its back on apartheid. But the Rothko Chapel that honored him with a special award stands in Harris County, "Death Penalty Capital of the World." Here, in my homeland, the poll takes the toll, and both *climb*.

Walking, now, back to the car, my sense of the chapel itself is still very much with me, its quiet inspiration pulling insistently at my mind. For if the Rothko chapel is not *merely* a receptacle for established religious visions; if the shape of space and color of the paintings themselves speak, silently but persuasively, of a *distinctive* vision, a form of revelation prepared by tradition and yet—at the same time— utterly without antecedent and so a *new birth* . . . if one can imagine this, then the *content* of that vision would, I think, be spiritually and practically bound to the historic cause of abolition, the eradication of the sentence of death that—to a mind inspired by the peculiar spiritual quality of the place—will inevitably appear sacrilegious. For the death penalty is the historical occlusion (not of the light but) of the dark vision of death's fateful portal, of the spiritual *initiation* that could work to release a people, a nation, a land, from the prisonhouse of fear, so that they might once more walk as children on the historic shore of a New World, pilgrims of the dawn.

A word then, (for I will conquer it),
The word final, superior to all,
Subtle, sent up—what is it?—I listen;
Are you whispering it, and have been all the time, you sea-waves?
Is that it from your liquid rims and wet sands?

Whereto answering, the sea,
Delaying not, hurrying not,
Whisper'd me through the night, and very plainly before daybreak,
Lisped to me the low and delicious word death,
And again death, death, death, death,
Hissing melodious, neither like the bird nor like my arous'd
*   child's heart,*
But edging near as privately for me rustling at my feet,
Creeping thence steadily up to my ears and laving me softly all over,
Death, death, death, death, death.

Which I do not forget,
But fuse the song of my dusky demon and brother,
That he sang to me in the moonlight on Paumanok's gray beach,
With the thousand responsive songs at random,
My own songs awaked from that hour,
And with them the key, the word up from the waves,
The word of the sweetest song and all songs,
That strong and delicious word which, creeping to my feet,
(Or like some old crone rocking the cradle, swathed in sweet garments,
bending aside)
The sea whisper'd me.

∼

DEATH SPEAKS

You know nothing of this harvest that
ties your loosened tongues. You have no ground
to hurl hate, or love, or wonder at
Death, whom the masqued women found

tragically disfigured within the mouth
of mourning. Yes, the world's still full of roles
unconsciously acted by imprisoned souls—
yes, chain-gangs still slave in the South.

But when we enter, a line of sunshine
stripes the stage, as if that silver hammer
struck gold in hell; heard the panting mine
scream: "spring Death from the slammer!"

But who hears? Mouths chewed by Fear,
they go on spitting sentences as though
they wrote the Book, as if they were seer
enough to take his part . . .

Hades: *What they don't know*
will kill them. Listen—I'm not the bonds-
man of some pale kind, but immortal King
of the Underworld, the black pond's
inky well, fount of the Stygian Spring.

Would you make this ghost-town land
brothel of justice? Hade's throne the tool
of some state-appointed stool? Remand
this moot court to a better law school.

As if a learned hand might cast a King
Pimp of Fear! Wait—I think I hear
a fairer sound; only the lyre-string
commutes my sentence. Hamlet, Lear—

all crown princes of the tragic past
are here with me forever, but one
comes and goes as if he would be mast-
er of these parts,
                 Hades'
dark son.

∾

Back in the offices of the Texas Resource Center and the Graham Coalition in the middle of the afternoon, the tension is terrible. Word could come through anytime now, though it is not expected for a few hours. There is nothing to do now, but wait. The workers at the Graham Coalition, the TRC lawyers, and all other human beings involved in this cause have done what they could do; now, it is out of their hands. Now, there is nothing to do but wait. Wait, and pray; pray, and keep faith.

I am sitting in the folding chair in the Texas Resource Center vestibule. The place is deadly quiet. Every once in a while someone emerges from one of the inner offices and walks like a somnambulist to the washroom in the hall. No one speaks.

There are several individuals here whom I have not seen before—an older Black couple and two teenagers. It does not take me long to realize who they are: Gary Graham's father and stepmother, his daughter Deirdre, and his son and namesake, little Gary. They know very well what is going on: they—all four of them—have been through this before: This is the third time that the state has scheduled the execution of their father or son, the third time the decision as to whether he will live or die has come down to the waning hours of the last day.

Time passes. Minutes stretch to hours, and the hours stretch on to endlessness.

How can one describe the character of time like that? It is not a simple thing. There is fear in it, and dread, a sense of desperate helplessness, a sense of a world out of control. One knows what is right, but one doesn't know, in the dreadful moments, if this matters at all. There, in the enclosed courtyard on the bottom floor where I have gone to rest, the green foliage of the small trees is etched in my mind; is carved as clearly as if the serrate outlines were cast in gold and worn in a chain around my neck. For there is something else there, too; something besides the fear and dread; something in the atmosphere that makes everything stand out in the mirror of mind; that prints every face, indelibly, upon the slate of memory. For, paradoxically, we human beings know immortality only in the presence of that which reminds us of our transience, only in the presence of the featureless face of death.

Aggrieved and exhausted, I am lying down, for a moment, in the courtyard; I am laying my long, slender body out upon the small concrete sidewall of the interior court fountain, I am laying myself down—I can do no more. My eyelids close for a moment—how long, I do not know—and when they open again, I am staring through space, up through the fingers of the trees, up into the dark chiseled faces of the two Black children who are leaning over the railing two short floors above, the son and daughter of the Black man who is, perhaps, about to die.

I am suspended over a well, I am looking into the depths of a pool, into a darkness that knows no bounds. Blue, beautiful blue water reflects the light. One sees an image—I see my image, there; but in the black, in the dark, in the well of those white eyes I see—*nothing*. I do not see anything in those eyes, in the eyes of the children. I have forgotten how to read.

A short while later, I ascend the stairs to the office, I pass them on the floor outside the office, there on the second floor. Deirdre is drawing. I see the figure of a bird in flight.

Ten minutes later, we hear the news. Though they had already moved him to the Death House, Gary Graham is not going to die—not tonight.

DEATH SENTENCE (SP II/9)

The head of the silver hammer builds death
row. When will the lock-jaw of the law
let my people go? Poem-breath
hangs in the air; the morning's raw.

The dreams of the dead lie with the earth like the sun
in shadow. Why wake and chain them to the chair
in the chamber? The corps of the blessed one
loves well-aged wine, not fermented fear.

And if he bloomed like a fresh bud from the bed
how could you ever sing that rose-red
body electric without remembering

this most terrible translation of his crowning sting?
Listen, the secret, silent saving sound
opens the ghost mouth

underground.

Buckingham Fountain

6

Coda:
A Poet's Parliament

Chicago, IL

You, neighbor God, when sometimes I wake you
with loud knocks in the night,
it is because I seldom
hear you breathe,
and know:
you
are alone
in the room.

And when you need something, there is no one
to put the drink into your hand:
I am always listening.
Send a little sign.
I am very
near.

Only a thin wall stands—
by chance—
between us; any moment, a cry
from your mouth or
from mine—
and it will fall
without a sound.

It is builded of your images.

And your images stand before you like names.
And then when the light inside me
through which I know you
in my being's depths
burns,

the brilliant glow is wasted
on your frames.

And my senses, so quickly
crippled, are
homeless,

and far

from you.

8/28 Chicago

It is the final day—the final night—of the Parliament of World Religions. People from all over the world, and all varieties of religious persuasion, have gathered here, in Chicago, to share their versions of spirit. My own summer's odyssey is drawing to a close —I am traveling back to Ithaca, my point d'appui—but stop here to catch, if I can, a glimpse of the future, the redeeming features of my kind.

Earlier today, I visited Chicago's Art Institute. I was reassured to find a body of Venus and a head of Mars still intact (though they were but Roman copies), and a variety of vessels that could still hold their wine. I did not see a medieval tapestry—any close cousin of my Lady and her Unicorn—but did not find this unsettling. Though I cannot, even now, in a single revelatory sentence, break the code of the mysterious connection vouchsafed me, three months before, in the Fine Arts Library at Cornell (wherever a true Lady is concerned, complete disclosure is out of the question), I do not think my Lady has been altogether reticent in her favors; trust that, all along, I have indeed been following her directions; have *made a beginning*, at least, at weaving the diverse strands of life and death into a colorful pattern that may catch the image of all *in you* that is most pure in heart.

Despite my Lady's absence, the Art Institute was hardly devoid of medieval inspiration today. I spent most of my time viewing a special exhibit called *Gates of Mystery: The Art of Holy Russia*. Russian icon painting—so closely bound to Orthodox theology— might seem infertile ground for more catholic imaginations of spirit, but I was pleasantly surprised to find that the meaning of the *icon* is not so easily contained within the frame of any one religious tradition. The very word marks— and crosses—the historic boundary between Greek philosophy and Christian theology, and while the name of the "anonymous author" of the following passage may be mere coincidence, one could hardly dispute that another privileged figure—the author of a "little book" called Nature—could readily have signed *his* name to the passage's bottom line:

> The word icon is derived from the Greek word for image (*eikon*) . . . Visible things are revealed images (*eikones*) of invisible things, declares an anonymous author of the 5th century, whose writing have survived under the name of Dionysios the Areopagite. What this means is that the material world is a single icon, and at the same time the sum total of icons.

And so, for a final time this summer, I found myself walking museum aisles, self-reflectively seeking images in the mirror of art. The work exhibited exquisite color and craftsmanship, but I was most fascinated by a formal device employed in many of the paintings. Here was an image of a saint, or (more commonly) the Blessed Mother and her Son, but the central figure was surrounded by a whole series of miniature scene-paintings, tiny tableaus narrating the pivotal events of the life. The little Byzantine "film strips" at the edge (reminiscent, in some respects, of my favorite Chartres windows), fractured the fixity of the dominant image, and it seemed to me that I could glimpse something of the hidden order of my own secret life in the scenarios of birth, death, and redemption shown there; that, indeed, all the colorful variations (here the "anastasis" figured in Christ's life-story, there, it did not) went so far as to invite more modern translations of the icon's archetypal motifs. Why, after all, should the *Fontaine-de-Vaucluse* not serve as well as the Jordan for a baptismal fount? And why should the reality of death row not substitute for priestly fantasies of the hellish side of Hade's dark domain? And—while the superstitious may flock to New Jersey suburbs at word of a "sighting" of the Virgin, why should not literary initiates see the weave of psyche's poetic text as a Marian incarnation?

Nor was it difficult to find traces of my mentor here, amidst the forest of Russian icons, for things Russian were hardly foreign to Rainer Maria Rilke. Around the turn of the century, traveling in tandem with a beloved companion, Rilke made two pilgrimages to the vast land and was deeply moved by the religious spirit he encountered there. In some wise, the book of prayers that resulted from that trip marked his advent as a poet whose own uniquely religious scripture figures an "original relation to the universe," a vision of the future indebted, but not indentured, to prior chapters in the book of human life. Was there ever a more appropriate time to read Rilke than now, as the millennium inscribes its approach in history's *Book of Hours*?

I live just as the century goes by.
One feels the wind from the great white page
where God and You and I have inscribed our age
and which strange hands turn over in the sky.

One feels the glow of a brand new leaf
upon which all may still take place.

Quiet powers draw arrows from a sheaf
and look each other darkly in the face.

SP II/22

Recall to me those early hours
when the trimmings of our sacred tree
were shooting stars and mountain flowers
and gemstones polished by the sea—

when the two of us were bound together
in the wind, and rain, and seething foam
a white sail, the strong flight feather
that helped us fly from ancient Rome.

Yet we were slaves, and will remain
until we face the foreign legion
ruling over earth and sea

as if these were provincial region
Ceasar's rightful ancestry
and Love's mast lost again.

It is evening, and the final program of the Parliament of Religions in progress. The large band shell in Chicago's Grant Park—across the street from the Art Institute, and near Lake Michigan's shore-line—hosts a crowd of thousands. The locale, at least, is familiar to me, for I am a native of this place, a child of The Windy City; and yet confess that tonight I feel like a stranger here, for I did not find a seat reserved for me at the Parliament of World Religions. Catholics and Protestants, Buddhists and Hindus, Jews and Muslims are privileged with name and place; nor did the progressive convention neglect Amerindian shamans, Wiccan, or the representatives of countless other less dominant spiritual species. Yet still I was left standing; there was no section set aside for more poetic figures, no acknowledged niche for a Petrarchan heir of Emerson inclined to regard "the Virgin Mary" as the unread text of R.M.R., and the *Sonnets to Orpheus* as living scripture, revelation, sacred psalm.

And yet, I am not out of place here, for a poet's platform is not so narrow as a parliament or park bench, and—even while keeping my own company—think I do have a hand in all that is going on. Early in the evening, the Dalai Lama spoke with wise humor of the quality of human life (the population explosion: "too much of a good thing"); then, the brightly colored plumage of an Amerindian troupe dipped and bobbed to the rhythmic beat of dancing feet. Now, a choir of gospel singers, young in body and soul, is filling the air with spiritual song.

I, meanwhile, have a rendezvous to keep. Leaving the crowd in the shell, I walk a little and am soon standing in a place reserved (after all) especially for me, for—like a certain vale of mountain flowers—I have known and loved it ever since I was a child. Rilke was fond of the small, circular, always flowing fountain that was, for him, a figure of faith, and the measure of his Muzot, but this big city boasts a larger basin within which to hold the holy waters of life. As the last chords pour forth from the band shell and fade into the night, Buckingham Fountain's great white flumes soar into space, and (as if celebrating the birth of a nation, or a new world) bloom into luminous sheets of color, into ever-falling leaves of glass.

And then (softly, lightly), it begins to rain.

SP II/21

> "This is
> stonecrop, this roseroot;
> this is live-forever."

> Scorning accident, the multicolored fountain
> geysers evenings in the greening park.
> True to genus, the flowers of the mountain
> shade the rough, pale, sharp-rising rock

> with painted parasols, as if that withering height
> were a sunny beach. And so the caved
> front of ruined temples, the blinded sight
> of antique eyes, is gradually lifted—saved

> my love, for you—for you, my love, and I.
> For others will circle the shooting water-fountain,
> and others will pick the flowers of the mountain

to analyze the dreamwork of the dye—
but we shall be the multicolored rain
that stains the stone-crop of the sky.

Postscript

The writing of this text reached its conclusion in Trumbull Corners, near Ithaca, N.Y., on August 31, 1995. On the evening of that day, its author attended an anti-death penalty vigil in front of the Ithaca post office. The next day, the death penalty was legally reinstated in the state of New York.

Construction of "the death house" is currently underway.

Orphica

Aphoristic Sayings

These Sayings are copied, largely verbatim, from the Note/Sketchbook the author carried on his travels. In general, the order of the entries reflects the order of composition. The category headings are not part of the original copy and are provided merely as a preliminary, heuristic guide to material that does not lend itself to rigid division. These aphorisms, moreover, are not intended to supply a comprehensive review or abstract of the body of the work: the "coverage" is uneven, and there are crucial topics in Rue Rilke not touched upon in these spontaneous jottings which—nonetheless—supplement the main text.

—the Author

Religion, Cosmogony, Art

Religion, in popular parlance, is not something one *is*, but that which one *"believes"*—which means, that which is beyond one, and towards which one gestures with a vain, almost hopeless hope. It is too often a premature surrender, a surrender out of ignorance, and not intelligence, of human limits. The only one who can, in good conscience, "surrender" to that which exceeds the human is the one who has tested its bound.

*

Each major realization of an art (a Rodin, a Rilke) implies a distinct version of creation; a configuration of divine and human energy, a casting of the roles of "god," "man," "woman," and "nature" in creation. The creative life of the human being is the true and actual worship, for it is present participation in the life and nature of god—not vain hope or wish that "God" cannot employ. It is, simultaneously, the means of the human self's own transfiguration:its transitions, evolutions, metamorphoses; its aspirations to the Good; its I-making, soulshaping, self-culture.

*

Creation is ongoing. It is not something accomplished once and for all, or over and done with. To be sure, the sky, the earth, do in some wise "exist," but not for us. We do not experience what we carelessly call "the creation"—God's world. We experience the earth, the world, covered with History; what man has made of the divine gift of being . . . here. Our proper work is to participate in the re-creation, the remaking of the world; and to do it with Love. This is the recipe for revolution. Redemption is not the work of a "savior" who might lift us all off this plane so many seem so anxious to leave, but rather the effect of innumerable individual acts of love and knowledge—of knowledgeable love—that carry, too, the currency of power; meet the gold-standard, pay in coin minted in darkness.

Spiritual History

The disdain for "earthly life" characteristic of much western religion is a gross misunderstanding of the processes of creation. "There is a different sun than the one in the sky." Creation is birthing from the earth womb-tomb; the re-arising or resurrection of history . . . in poetry.

*

Humankind has gone through the Seven Ages unconsciously; it is now our task to recollect history—to recall it, and thus make a new beginning. "History" has always been a masculine affair; we would have it be . . . a love affair.

*

The Earth is a Great Book always in the process of revision.

*

"Man" has lived upon the Earth without cognizance of his ground. He has built his cities on flood-plains, his industries in the midst of old-growth forest. His words are not things, and the current events of his life transpire out of all relation to eternal concerns. He does not know the characters that compose his Self. Our humanity is not given, but is an attainment—but modern man is a spiritual underachiever. We are "the little people"—without magic.

*

In the Middle Ages, the social, religious, and political aspects of life were closely integrated. One had a place in the spiritual-religious world, and a correspondent one in the sociopolitical order. God was God, kings were kings, peasants and guildworkers, peasants and guildworkers. The individual was taken up, absorbed in these structures. Although they may have been, in many respects, terribly oppressive, there was definition, placement in a larger order that soared up to "God." And "God" was present—part of everyday life, woven into the rhythms and rituals of work, the fabric of feeling.

Today, we do not have this God. Our "God" is a god of wish-fulfillment. Religious feeling does not come to original expression in our temples; does not work in the loom of our life. "Religion," in mainstream America, is disfigured into social clubbing and a mindless moralism that is a throwback to our Puritan past. However, at its most zealous, our "religion" does attain a murderous intensity worthy of the "Dark Ages." Religion today, is not *positively*, but *negatively*—feudal, displaying some of the worst features of the medieval world, and none of the best.

*

What I am interested in is the human character, and the character of the human, in a given historical moment. Or has "history"—as a concept, a construct, already predetermined our notion of "the human?" How do we see human being, how envision, construe, perceive that which we "authentically" are, how extract this from—as Rilke writes in one letter—the layers of history? I am interested, too, in the changing definitions, characterizations of the Artist, and the position of the artist and his production in society.

By and large, for the medieval artist, art remains subordinated to theology. For Dante, and even Petrarch, the work of art remains, to a significant degree, within a pre-established religious (Christian) world view. Within that cosmos, there is great freedom, but the cosmos is create, is given. The medieval is the apogee of the Christian worldview, and its organization in terms of religious hierarchy and social code.

With the Renaissance, there is a loosening of the hold of the church. Renaissance humanism looks back to the classical world, and yet of course established religious structure and cosmology remains extremely powerful. Galileo is born the same year as Shakespeare. Are Shakespeare's "mystery plays"?

With Romanticism, the focus on the individual psyche or subject, and their mode of so-called "self-consciousness" is extraordinarily intensified, and set loose from established theological structure. This is, one must note, a moment of revolutionary promise, and yet the situation is inherently unstable, since the psychological subject alone is not an adequate container for the panoply of forces historically embedded in religion and social code. Romanticism marks a critical juncture in the life of the spirit, and leaves as its legacy this question: can the authority absorbed and internalized into/by the individual psyche/ subject (archetypically represented by the artist or poet-hero) be sustained and redistributed into social forms that can preserve the sanity of the subject, and carry forward the revolutionary impulse into renovated forms of culture? Or will that impulse fall back into the lap of old and new forms of the hegemony of the collective over the individual?

The modern period is inaugurated by the dynamics of alienation and emptiness. The structures of self-consciousness perhaps did not achieve intersection with reigning political and religious structure; the Romantic spirit did not succeed in generating a culture that embodied its salient values. The utopian urges implicit in Romanticism (including the great political revolutions) broke down under various pressures. The horizon of modernity is— death.

Against what background do we see—*paint*—the character of our kind?

Gesamtwerk

The different arts exemplify different modes of liberation and realization, or embodiment of spirit. These are grounded in the concrete materials and methods characteristic of the arts. In **sculpture**, one begins with the unformed rock, and must cut away the mass of stone to reveal the form locked inside. In **painting**, one begins with a white canvass, and form and figure is built up from line and color. In **photography**, the image found is an extract of life, and the art consists primarily in capturing the moment in a fitting frame, and the subsequent development of the image from the negative—negotiations of light and darkness. Photography is the unit of **film**, but cinema emphasizes the sequential arrangement of the image, the splicing of the frames. In **dance**, we begin with the body and its fluid potential; the art is a matter of a bending, turning, living permutation of the human form and its expressive potential. **Architecture** is the materialization of space. **Music** begins with the substance and order of sound; composing involves transcribing the sequences that correspond with the state of soul embodied in the tone. **Speech** is much like music, but the body of the word . . . **Calligraphy** is the dance of the hand, for letters are characters of consciousness, miniatures of memory, the mind's toys.

All the other art forms inhabit the Art of the Letter. **Orphic Theatre**, ideally, would be a virtual synthesis of many, if not all, art forms; a true **Gesamtwerk**. Such a synthesis is a theoretical possibility because all the diverse languages of art are really various facets of a single language (rooted in the living body) which is the substructure of all the beautiful phenomena through which spirit makes itself known. Spirit manifests itself in and through poetry (here conceived in the widest possible sense; the poetic element in all), for the poetic is the medium of revelation. Needless to say, poetic disclosure is never complete.

The Individual

We do not understand—what is the Individual. The School's emphasis on "the social construction" of identity makes the Individual subordinate to objectified and objectifying collective forces. The individual attainment to art always involves a decisive break from the sphere of the social, which break opens the possibility (otherwise closed) of assimilating the circumambient lines of social force to the poetry of soul. Poetic nature and agency is not to be *derived* from the social factors that are its milieu and its material, any more than the magic of alchemy can be reduced to the elements of chemical equation.

*

The horizon of our kind is defined by the value of the Individual. But church Christianity denies the individual his or her own unique relation to divinity. You are not supposed to grow into God by the fullness of your human being, by the exfoliation of all your faculties, but by obeisance to the cult that deifies the person of Jesus. The battle between the poet and the church has been joined—by the Romantics, by Emerson, by Rilke—but is as yet undecided. It must be joined again. And it is not primarily a question of accepting or rejecting Christ—but the terms that constitute true spiritual inheritance of the wisdom and love of this great teacher. The church owns no special rights to his mystery play.

*

The idea that individual participates in God only through the Christ-nature is a valid teaching, but the exclusive identification of the person of Jesus with the Christ-nature is not. Then, instead of becoming an object of contemplation that aids the Individual in their own realization of the Christ-nature, figurations of Christ become blocks and barricades to the spiritual imagination: a bolt across the door of the soul. The great friend of humanity is made into its arch-enemy.

Exegesis

In connection with the Christian impulse, we must go back to the SPIRITUAL MEANING of the LIVES of CHRIST and MARY. All else is secondary and derivate; all else is history.

*

We have a whole history of interpretation of the figure of Christ, but this history starts off on the wrong foot. The Church offers a literalistic reading of the sacred passion narrative, preaching creed, belief, and faith instead of first-hand knowledge of the laws of the soul. It sets religious symbol in stone, but (unlike the work of the Greeks) this is not *living* sculpture.

*

It was never "God" that was dead, but the religious imagination, which is not exactly the same thing.

*

What Christ performed religiously needs to be *repeated,* but with a difference—in a manner that is simultaneously historical-material, philosophical, psychological, poetical.

Dream reading

Sacred history is the dream of the Earth. Religio-political history is its waking nightmare.

*

Creation, now, is not *ex nihilo;* it is a transformation of inherited memories. Creation proceeds in accordance with the logic of the dream, which coincides with the logic of literary history, poetically construed.

*

Poetry is redeemed history. "Redemption" is not liberation from the laborious travail and sensual pleasure of earthly life, but realization or actualization of the life of the Earth in and through the creative life of the human soul, which proceeds in accord with the logic of compensation.

*

In poetic life, historical or legendary events are remembered; rescripted, replayed *differently,* in accord with the spirit of the times. To interpret an event cannot mean to take it literally; the literal is the moment of inscription. *Reading* takes place on plane of the figure.

*

Fundamentalism is almost always premised upon literalism, and a monopolization of the meaning of sacred scripts by arbitrary ideological fiat. The institution of the church is a (sometimes mild) form of fundamentalism.

Spiritual Economy

Christian theology alienates the Soul from nature and from labor. Love— "God"—is divorced from Nature, from her labor and travail. My labor is not "rewarded" by "God"; it is (of) "God"; it requires no reward, but rather *good exchange.*

*

Mainstream Christianity and capitalism co-exist all too comfortably. In the U.S., we see something of a *church economy* (the alienation, through hierarchal mediation, of labor from God/love).

*

Reverence for God—for the infinite—is revealed only through realization of the finite. The concrete works that contribute to this realization are the means by which we are *employed* by God. The heart of religion is *the exchange of goods* that carry Love's dedication.

Psyche

What are the laws of love and beauty; the conditions of our participation in these forms of grace? We need stories, books, which speak to the recreation of our world out of ourselves, for in this, each Psyche is a Virgin Mary.

*

The creativity of Woman is somehow outside history; at the same time, it is the ground of a more truly *human futurity.*

*

Psyche has been *man-handled* by Science. Has she ever been truly *loved?*

*

Humanity is renewed, rebirthed from out of its own *travail.* Such a *conception* is neither the Genesis of "our Father," nor the heavenly "salvation" of the soul.

*

Soul-life has been confined to "psychology" while the circumambient energies of the world and divinations of the mind have been left out of "psychology." In psychology, we've had a hundred years of solitude. (Or is it co-dependency?)

Eros, Anima, Aphrodite, Aesthetics

At present, "God" has no face. People lift their hopes up . . . "to Him"—yet do not know him, or understand the relation of divine power to the human being. "God" is invoked to stand in for truth, value, and responsibility; but the moral prescriptions that characterize "his" discourse does not build upon an ethic of Love, and is impotent in the face of the energies and forces of Nature it fails to incorporate within the life of Spirit. Puritan morality knows nothing of Psyche, and despises Eros: is premised upon a FEAR of Nature. It does not understand the difficult dialectic of the conversion of natural into spiritual life proper to the masculine and feminine psyches.

*

The call for a return to "values" in the name of religion is doomed to miserable failure since the inherited religious frameworks are part of the problem. Historical Christianity, in particular, fails to integrate the dark, the shadow, the energies of Eros and of Psyche instrumental to the creative life of the individual. That creative life is the basis upon which progressive civilization rests, for it is only through development of our full humanity, manifesting itself in the employment and harmonizing of God-given faculties, that the human being stands in good relation to "God" or "the Gods"; to Nature; and (the economy of love) enjoys fair exchange with others of his and her kind.

*

The word "love" is rife with ambiguity and multiple in reference. If we were to categorize, in a gross way, kinds of love, we might mention: 1) love between individual human beings (friendship and erotic relationship); 2) *"Allgemeines Menschenliebe"* or the human being's (transpersonal) love for the whole of its kind; 3) the love between the human and that which transcends the mortal estate; e.g. "God," "the Gods," angels; 4) love of all the things of Nature, or the Creation (animal, vegetable, mineral and the all the things of beauty man and woman make from and with these things).

Now, what is crucial in Rilke's vision is that the "highest" variety (divine love) is not ultimately separable from the lowest (creature-thing love), because the continual arising of things into life (through poetic nature, its mediation) is the primary activity of divine love in the earthly sphere—this *bearing*. Whereas, in the realm of God the Father, the creative manifestation of things (born of pain, travail, labor as exemplified or realized in the work of art) is not considered the primary activity of the divine; indeed, it is not, in general, part of our conception of God the Father. For Him, the primary channel of divine agency is abstract Law, Judgment, Commandment . . . writ in stone. This Law was perhaps sufficient to sustain the religious consciousness in a patriarchal order of things; but it is wholly insufficient today, when the human being is in a quite different state of development, and when the equality of Man and Woman is generative of the idea of the New World.

*

In our "Christian" culture, we do not think that "God" includes the body, especially the feminine body. Thus we do not understand that perception of the beauty of that body— incarnate, at one level, in the body of woman, and, at another, as that of the Earth (the entirety of nature) is integral to religious consciousness; and that learning to love that body is . . . religious education. This, in turn, requires *aesthetic education*.

*

In the Alyscamps: One way of looking at the resurrection: this is the re-arising of *phenomena* in(to) *things*; the conversion of natural life into the flowers of creation—we could say, into "art." This is the work of love, which in turn is premised upon death, insofar as it is only on the "other side" of death—its emptiness, its nullity and negation—that love is *free*.

*

The laws of art are the laws of love, and form the basis upon which religious knowledge rests. To preach religious truth without psychological and aesthetic truth is to raise the roof of a temple before laying the foundation, or building the supporting pillars of stone.

*

Fontaine-de-Vaucluse: The love that the (Petrarchan) lover sees in his lady is a reflected light, its source divine Eros "in" him. Yet the lover requires the mirror of the other to experience the power of love. But this does not mean that the beloved is a dispensable adjunct, for no lover is Love, and to deny the object of affection an original and co-equal role is uncommon hubris. For, even if the light of love is a reflected light, the glass must be good: the beauty of the beloved is not some seductive ploy of a beguiling Nature, but rather the prepared-ness of the feminine soul to receive the shaping idea(l)s projected by the lover. The classical "mistake," however—constitutive of the tradition—is to make the human object the locus of ideality, rather than a reality that at one and the same time confirms ideality in its own peculiar beauty, and *also* acts as a locus of reality that resists and even denies idealization. This only transpires when the intercourse between partners achieves real psychological depth, and involves a mutually beneficial relation to the transference of spiritual energies between the pair. Traditional psychological theory, however, gives no purchase on this, because it is not based upon the premises of love and beauty, or the irreducible, transcendental ideality contributed by Eros. The art of love, of psyche-ology, is to maintain a dialectical tension between the transcendental ideal contributed by the primordially masculine impetus (and this would include the relation to the divine intellect or *nous* mediated by love), and the soul-force incarnate in Psyche. This is the heart of soul-making.

*

The efficacy of the processes of love depends upon the culture of the lover—and, most particularly, his capacity to *"language love"*: to trans-late the transcendental insight inherent in Love's vision into lines that transmit that intelligence to Psyche, "inseminate" or animate Psyche. It depends, equally, upon the capacity of Psyche to receive, reflect, germinate, gestate, and *bear* the fruit of love. And: the enlivening, spiritualizing force does not "belong" only to eros; for in some wise, psyche—as anima—is always already instinct (impregnated) with divine life, and has absorbed and transmuted this in the ground of her character. Thus, whereas Psyche may take on a more passive aspect in relation to divine Eros, in real life, the masculine force is very often dis-spirited, or trapped in forms of lifeless intellectuality which look to Psyche, anima, for the vivification of imaginative activity. But Love will fail if the masculine principle does not realize its prior relation to divine Eros (and logos), just as it will fail if the feminine posits itself as passive and spiritless vis-a-vis the masculine, and so fails to act out of its own, quite distinct, spiritual character.

Wisdom

The telos of the feminine aspect of the soul cannot be simply identified with the transcendental ideality of Love, of Psyche's divine partner. The term of Psyche's own evolution, the "end" of her travails, is not simply vertical transcendence of herself (this would be to deny, to abandon her own essence) but Wisdom (Sophia), an immanent knowledge of space, time, matter, the ground of manifestation and transformation in Nature. This is material knowledge, in the deepest sense of the term.

*

The telos of the feminine aspect of soul is Sophianic wisdom; that of the masculine, the wisdom-consciousness of Dionysius-Christ. The transcendental intelligence of divine Eros must enter into contact with time, nature, history, mortality (all carried by psyche/anima), and "rise again" to reclaim a divinity that is now embodied, carnate, and pledged to Earth—to the healing of the Earth, its transfiguration. That cannot be accomplished without knowledge of death, temporality, and the concrete complexes composing the human historical moment.

*

We tend to think of a human life as bound between birth and death; defined, that is, by the formation and disintegration of the physical body. But there are other "deaths," e.g.:

—Psyche's "death": the withdrawal of psychic energy, of the soul, from the world (especially the familial and social world) to become the bride of Eros.

—the crucifixion: symbolically, the self-sacrifice or death of the ego, as the soul assumes karmic responsibility for the plight of its kind. This involves actually *taking upon itself* the complexes characterizing the collective, so as to enable a moment of transformation impossible if these energies are simply negated or excluded from the realm of spirit.

Contemporary Culture

The schism between those discourses which would uphold traditional values and the relativistic impetus of multiculturalism etc. is, in significant degree, the "death of Eros"—the failure to integrate Love (and Love's body) into the intellectual and psychological fabric of our lives, our (un)common culture.

*

Politics and the discourse of power has become the God of the Schools; but we have no ethical relationship to this power, since we have dispensed with Beauty, and all the intellectual forms by which it is related to the Good. We have sacrificed the Ideal on the altar of the Real, and batten on the corpse of culture.

*

What we are experiencing in America is the upsurge of failure of our spiritual inheritance. This includes, on the one hand, the tradition of the church and state (implying separation of religion and politics, which is only possible when "religion" is characterized by the creed of an institutionalized form); and, on the other hand, the failure of American Schools effectively to inherit *and transform*—in accordance with New World vision—the intellectual and cultural legacy of Europe, which cannot be simply *rejected* in favor of a less "Eurocentric" ideology.

*

The doctrine of the separation of church and state posits, in principle, separate spheres for (1) administration of secular affairs and government of the polity; and (2) the life of the spirit. This is conceivable, from the religious standpoint, on account of Christian cosmology, which drives a wedge between heaven and earth, time and eternity, temporal and eternal life.

*

What is happening in America—is the breakdown of established, traditional orders, mores, morals. Within the university, there is recognition that established power structures have been complicit in appropriative and dominating forms of thought and rule. There is the belief, as well, that the canon of western literature has been complicit in such ideology, even while sometimes contesting it. The traditional order has been sexist, racist, classist . . . so that there is a need to make room for other voices; those that have historically been "marginalized."

Diversity becomes a chief value, multiculturalism a new ideology. Yet, even if we freely admit the liberating impulse contained in such initiatives, it is necessary to ask: how is the "new order'" reached, actualized? How clear, how comprehensive—with respect to the human spirit—is the "vision" offered by this new ideology? Is it built upon a solid spiritual foundation, a comprehensive knowledge of the nature of (the archetypal nature of) human being?

*

There is a Dionysian impulse in America— towards diversity, libidinal liberation—but where is the Apollonic complement that would contribute to a fruitful dialectic? What form, order, pattern can the new impulses take to be most constructive? What relation to the "old," the traditional canon? We need new literatures with roots in history, mythology, religion, which effect a transformation of the inherited order of western culture and value; otherwise its rejection (in the name of what?) leads to a loss of creative tension, and to dis-integrating schism in the body politic; a polarization of senex and puer.

Death Penalty

What is this mania for capital punishment? Is it a considered demand for justice? What rules is Fear—and I think we can say that Americans have failed to integrate darkness and death into the psyche, into the ecology and economy of "the American Mind" (if there is any such thing). This may well have something to do with that most troublesome symptom of America's ill-health: *racism.*

*

In America, is death color-blind?

*

Houston Bed and Breakfast: Yesterday a revolutionary thought occurred to me. Why not exhort the community of scholars to conform idea to deed, and incite the PC to action? I mean: since capital punishment is antithetical to Reason; represents an eclipse of intelligence; since it is a critical organ of oppression continuous with the history of abused power against which the academy arrays itself, is it not the responsibility of the citizen-scholar to oppose this, to fight this institution, even unto the death? If literary criticism has become obsessed with the politics to the point of making power relations the ground of its understanding of human character, does the critic mean to contend that this is necessarily an a- or immoral and violent reality? (That is pure Nietzscheanism.) To be sure, a certain kind of violence may be inherent in the political organization of humankind, a certain species of bondage. But is there not, as well, potential power in the political agency that does not consort with the system of social violence; agency, that is, which draws power from the Good, and the spiritual laws of the soul?

Surely, surely—though the academy has grown quite unaccustomed to such transcendentalist inflection—it does hold that one can draw certain lines between good and evil, because the political impulse in the academy grows out of ethical imperative, is moralizing in the extreme.

Indeed, this precisely the problem: the ethical impetus associated with "PC" runs the risk of overdrive, of solidifying into pure ideology; and *there is no truly literary ethics.* The academy plies its trade, largely unconscious of—and inarticulate about—its own premises, and this intellectual failure translates into a political failure: the community of scholars fail to seize initiative in connection with issues such as capital punishment, and so do not begin to realize its potential political power, its capacity to inform public discourse, debate, and imagination.

The Player Piano

Château de Muzot: The so-called "senses" are not, correctly conceived, organs of purely phenomenal experience, and the association of the senses with purely empirical experience is one of those benighted *faux pas* symptomatic of Man's chronic inability to move in and domicile himself in his own house—"the body," if you will. Our ordinary sense experience, which delivers to us mere phenomena, is the work of underfed, uneducated senses: senses that have not been cultivated in such a way as to empower an entirely different quality of perception— which is as purely "spiritual" as the contemplation of immaterial ideas. Our undernourished senses are rather like some precious old piano—intact but begrimed—we might find in a junk heap, and most of what passes for human life naught but the discordant tunes of one who found the instrument, but did not bother to clean or care for it, and so reclaim its original action, but, forthwith, went around the world with this old impossible instrument strapped to his back. And of course we might well imagine that it gets beat up still more along history's old road, so that at last the ill-treated clavier can do nothing but shriek, whine and whimper, and make music that sounds like the gnashing of teeth.

Philosophy and religion in the West give inadequate aid to our poor traveler. Indeed, too much of the time, the catechism amounts to little more than this profound advisory, phrased in a hundred different ways: "cast off the piano, friend, so you can stand up and see the sky, and hear the sounds of heaven pouring forth from the mouths of angels." But is it not evident what awful ignorance and hubris this foists upon the human soul? As if we might be admitted to the realm of celestial sound and the deep harmonies of the divine before even bothering to tune our own instrument, or learn the scales that score the songs of our lives.

And it will be further understood that heavenly music, strictly speaking, is but a myth, and the harmony man has always sought in heaven does not, in fact, exist there, for in heaven there is no time or space in which the notes might unfold. To be sure, ravishing beauty exists in the celestial sphere, but it is the beauty of the score or the staff, not the performance itself, which must always be of the nature of an *event*. But it is well known that nothing ever happens in heaven; that is the key to its peculiar bliss.

The spiritual event that is, too, the advent of the new and renewed world, occurs in the interchange between the angelic and heavenly host—consciousnesses allied with the supratemporal, supra-spatial realm of immortal reality—and the transient and ever changing truth of the mortal human psyche. That event—in reality a series of events, without beginning, without end—is the poem of the Soul.

And so finally here, in view of the *Château de Muzot,* I begin to understand something of the meaning woven into the beautiful tapestries of *The Lady and the Unicorn,* each one of which (with one singular exception) is associated with one of the five senses. Do not these indicate just how little we know of the wisdom proper to the feminine figure? Feminism—in its present theoretical and social formations— does not touch upon this, but is a mere spin-off of the canonical history of conceptuality and power (it is good to investigate the Lady's social position, but one must also *listen* to the music she plays). And the religious tradition, the main thrust of Christianity, denies our human beauty at its very source, its native station. The tapestries point beyond history to Christ's mythic prefigurations; back and beyond to Orpheus and Eurydice; to the truth of beauty construed— not only in religious and moral aspect—but, more basically, in connection with the aesthetic premise of our participation in the world of Love.

There is nothing more *gross* than the violence that afflicts our society, nothing more *gross* than the antidotes we prescribe, nothing nearly so gross—morally, physically— as the institution of capital punishment, which—wholly blind to the deeper, spiritual meaning of death, inevitably blinds us to the meaning of life, and the merciful ground of love. Who could think of Vera's death without seeing the ineluctable link between death, beauty, and immortal life? Who can doubt that so long as we chain the spirit in the crude logic of vengeance, its delicate dance-like expressions will be unable to dwell with us, and will be taken into the arms of death like some ancient human sacrifice to compensate the God of the Underworld for all the horror we are forcing down his throat?

If we are to reenter, rediscover, reinvent a truly human world, a civilized world where love abides, we need find different premises for our society—its education, economy, culture, government—premises and sensibilities not fully unfolded in the Bible, or at least in the more popular figurations of the Father-God and his moral commandment. A true ethic is arrived at— not by way of imperative, but by becoming versed in the forms of beauty which naturally cultivate a regard for life and experience of value, so that standards of conduct emerge—not through externally imposed pre- and proscription, blind obeisance, and willed "faith"— but from the felt experience of love, and the reality of beauty in human life.

~

KKK Grand Dragon, Huntsville, Texas (Scott Langley)

Afterword

Gary Graham was first scheduled for execution in 1987. In 1993, Graham was "scheduled" three times. A 30-day reprieve granted by Texas Governor Ann Richards spared Graham's life in April; *Rue Rilke* narrates the circumstances of his narrow escapes in June and August of that year. Graham—or rather Shaka Sankofa, for such was the name Graham officially took in 1995—received another "date" in January 1999, but once more litigation temporarily staved off his execution *without, however, securing the right to introduce new evidence into formal court proceedings.*

Shaka Sankofa received yet another date the following year. In May of 2000, the United States Supreme Court ruled by a vote of 5 to 4 to uphold a lower court decision refusing him the right to further judicial review on the basis of the so-called Anti-Terrorism and Effective Death Penalty Act—an act passed well *after* the filing of Graham/Sankofa's petition to secure such review. Shortly after the Supreme Court's decision, Texas Governor George W. Bush signed a new death warrant. In so doing, Bush brushed aside pleas for clemency issuing from all corners of the globe, including an "Appeal to Decency" authored by the International Secretariat of Amnesty International and a full-page ad in *The New York Times* signed by six former death row inmates who had been found innocent and ultimately released.

Civil Disobedience, Austin, Texas
(Scott Langley)

On the night of June 22, 2000, hundreds of protesters gathered outside the prison in Huntsville, Texas, where Shaka Sankofa was to be executed. A sizable contingent of police kept apart those gathered on Sankofa's behalf from others (including members of the KKK) present to support his execution. Inside the prison, Shaka Sankofa actively resisted his impending execution so that authorities found it necessary to dispatch a cell extraction team to transport him forcibly to the execution chamber. Once this had been accomplished, it required five guards to strap him to the gurney. Gary Graham/Shaka Sankofa died of lethal injection at 8:49 p.m. on June 22, 2000.

Six days later, on June 28, roughly 2000 people attended his wake.

Before his death, Shaka Sankofa issued a final statement that begins as follows:

> I would like to say that I did not kill Bobby Lambert. That I'm an innocent black man that is being murdered. This is a lynching that is happening in America tonight. There's overwhelming and compelling evidence of my defense that has never been heard in any court of America. What is happening here is an outrage for any civilized country to anybody anywhere to look at what's happening here is wrong.
>
> I thank all of the people that have rallied to my cause . . . . We must continue to move forward and do everything we can to outlaw legal lynching in America. We must continue to stay strong all around the world, and people must come together to stop the systematic killing of poor and innocent black people. We must continue to stand together in unity and to demand a moratorium on all executions. We must not let this murder/lynching be forgotten.

Since the summer of 1993 and, subsequently, Shaka Sankofa's execution in 2000, some change has transpired while much has stayed the same. A wave of highly publicized incidents of violence against Black men and women over the last year or so has brought matters of race and social justice roaring to the forefront of American consciousness once again, garishly illuminating the systemic racial prejudice that still pervades American life, breeding continual tragedy. Correlatively, the death penalty remains the law of the land in a majority of states, and well over 1,000 persons have been executed since the completion of *Rue Rilke* 20 years ago. One recent case in particular reveals how (in certain respects, at least) virtually nothing seems to have changed in this country's capital punishment profile.

His (White) race aside, many aspects of Richard Glossip's case bear telling resemblances to that of Gary Graham. Glossip, a motel manager accused of arranging the murder of the motel's owner (Barry Van Treese) in Oklahoma City in 1997, was convicted and sentenced to death for that crime in 2004. After various lengthy proceedings, Glossip was first scheduled for execution on January 29, 2015. His case, like Graham's, represents an instance in which the courts and relevant governor (Mary Fallin) repeatedly brushed aside strong evidence of innocence; or—at the very least—reasonable doubt as to his guilt. Glossip, after all, was convicted on the basis of the testimony of the man—Justin Sneed—who actually *performed* the murder in question, and Sneed's testimony spared Sneed the prospect of capital prosecution. A July 19, 2015, article in the online journal *The Intercept* states:

> From the police interrogation of Justin Sneed in 1997 to transcripts from Glossip's two trials, the picture that emerges is one of a flimsy conviction, a case based on the word of a confessed murderer with a very good incentive to lie, and very little else.

As in Graham's case, the initial phases of Glossip's defense were hamstrung by egregiously deficient legal counsel. As in Graham's case, too, high-profile figures (Sister Helen Prejean,

Susan Sarandon, even Pope Francis) ultimately rallied to Glossip's cause. Even so, despite several temporary reprieves (Glossip ordered a last supper three separate times), Glossip's saga would have ended in tragedy if had not been for a novel twist of fate, a niggling circumstance that reveals a widening crack in the American institution of capital punishment.

Pharmaceutical companies within the United States are refusing to provide drugs for death; nor can such be readily obtained abroad. Due to the paucity of drugs thus legally available, Oklahoma had already staged one botched execution, a highly publicized fiasco that resulted in prolonged torture of the victim. It is hardly surprising, then, the Glossip's lawyers recently argued that Oklahoma's death penalty represented unconstitutionally cruel and unusual punishment. This appeal was heard by the United States Supreme Court which—in a 5 to 4 verdict issued on June 29, 2015—rejected Glossip's argument. Justice Samuel Alito's chillingly merciless opinion begins: "Because capital punishment is constitutional, there must be a constitutional means of carrying it out."

Despite that decision, the state of Oklahoma itself called off Glossip's execution an hour before it had been (re)scheduled to take place at 3 p.m. Wednesday, September 30. Why? It was discovered that Oklahoma did not in fact have any potassium chloride—one of the three requisite lethal injection drugs prescribed by its protocol—but only potassium acetate, a food preservative that did *not* qualify as a legal alternative, and the use of which could have resulted in yet another nightmarish death house scenario. Not only was Glossip's execution delayed, but, as of October 2, 2015, Oklahoma indefinitely postponed all executions in order to give it time to investigate its problematical drug dilemma.

As I wrote the first draft of this *Afterword* in July of this year, Richard Glossip's life hung in the balance—just as Gary

Graham's did as I began *Rue Rilke* in the summer of 1993. Now, it appears likely that Glossip (unlike Graham) will still be alive when this book appears, and so—even though much of Glossip's case can be seen as disheartening evidence that little has changed on the death penalty front—one can also see in it indications of the opposite, more encouraging truth.

For the winds of change *are* blowing—and more and more stiffly, too—with respect to capital punishment. A June 24, 2015, *Washington Post* article cites a number of revealing statistics: while a slim majority of the U.S. citizenry still supports the death penalty, that majority has been eroding since the mid-1990s; while 31 states as well as the federal government still have the death penalty on the books, one-third of the 19 states that have abolished it have done so since 2007; while only China, Iran, Saudi Arabia, and Iraq execute more persons than the United States of America, this country saw far fewer death sentence and executions (35) in 2014 than in preceding years. Such data led the *Post* bluntly to state: "The death penalty is on the decline in the U.S."

Another important recent development—one profoundly relevant to many *Rue Rilke* reflections—may help hasten that decline. The *Post* article was in fact prompted by Pope Francis' historic address to Congress in the course of which Francis declared his unequivocal support for the cause of abolition. Boldly advocating "global abolition of the death penalty," Francis offered "encouragement to all those who believe that a just and necessary punishment must never exclude the dimension of hope and the goal of rehabilitation."

Abolitionists across the globe welcomed the pope's words; not so Catholic Supreme Court Justice Antonia Scalia, who stands as one prominent member of a legal system that more often than not continues to prop up the capital punishment scarecrow.

A glance at the cast of other characters involved in the unfolding drama of social justice in the USA reveals elements of both constancy and change in this regard as well. Hillary Rodham Clinton, the first lady to whom I addressed my letter on Graham's behalf in 1993, remains front and center in the public eye and may end up re-entering the White House as the first woman president of the United States. Minister Louis Farrakhan, whose impassioned speech I heard in the basement of the Hyatt Regency in the dog days of that long-ago Houston summer, endures as the head of the Nation of Islam. Just a few months ago, on July 30, 2015, Farrakhan, speaking in a Miami church, delivered an incendiary message regrettably contrary to the one delivered 22 years ago in Houston. This charged counterpoint may serve to illustrate that Gary Graham's story—indeed, the whole mosaic of poetic, philosophic, and political reflection composing *Rue Rilke*—remains intensely relevant today.

I will end on a literary note. In the fall of 2000, the year that Shaka Sankofa was executed, *Dead Man Walking*—an opera based on Sister Helen Prejean's book by that same name—premiered in San Francisco. After attending a performance of the opera, I wrote the following pantoum, which I would here like to rededicate to the memory of those (including Gary Graham/Shaka Sankofa) who have been executed in the United States of America and to the abolitionist cause that continues to seek to stem that violent tide.

Dead Man Walking

The machine whirrs
while a man lies stretched out upon a cross-shaped gurney.
The violins and trumpets are speechless.
The machine debuts its hoarse death-rattle: *click, whirr, click,*
whirr, click . . .

Rue Rilke

A man lies stretched out upon a cross-shaped gurney
like many before him.
The machine debuts its hoarse death rattle: *click, whirr, click,*
whirr, click . . .
Black milk flows through its arms.

Like many before him,
the man strains hard against the thongs that strap him down.
Black milk flows through his arms.
He lifts and twists his head,

strains hard against the thongs that strap him down—
but his blood drinks the black milk; the black milk's in his mouth.
He lifts and twists his head
(that darkening gaze, those half-wild eyes)

but his blood drinks the black milk; the black milk's in his mouth.
And we—we—are the witnesses. We watch
that darkening gaze, those half-wild eyes
while the machine sings its toneless solo center stage.

And we—we—are the witnesses. We watch
silently as his struggle slowly ceases,
and the machine sings its toneless solo center stage.
For Death is a master from . . .

Silently, his struggle slowly ceases.
He turns from us, he turns toward her,
for Death is a master from . . .
Drowned in black milk,

he turns from us, he turns toward her . . .
The machine whirrs;
drowned in black milk,
the violins and trumpets are speechless.

Good Friday procession to
women's death row, Raleigh, N.C. (Scott Langley)

Sources

Throughout the text, poems titled "**SO**" are the author's own early translations of one of Rilke's *Sonnets to Orpheus*. ("**SO II/15**" would designate Sonnet # 15 of Part II of Rilke's *Sonnets to Orpheus*.) For the author's recently published translation of the complete work, see the bilingual edition: Rilke, *Sonnets to Orpheus*, translated by Daniel Joseph Polikoff (Kettering, OH: Angelico Press, 2015).

Throughout the text, poems titled "**SP**" are poems in the author's own (unpublished) sonnet sequence, *Sonnets to Psyche*. These represent metamorphoses of Rilke's *Sonnets to Orpheus*. As work on *Sonnets to Psyche* did not always progress in order, the number of the transformed Rilke sonnet *may or may not* correlate with the number of the corresponding sonnet to Psyche.

All Rilke poems are translated by the author unless otherwise noted below.

All poems not otherwise identified below are the author's own (unpublished) work.

❦

Below, **MLB** stands for Rainer Maria Rilke, *The Notebooks of Malte Laurids Brigge,* trans. by M.D. Herter Norton (New York: W.W. Norton, 1949, 1977).

GN stands for *Letters of Rainer Maria Rilke, 1910-1926,* trans. by Jane Bannard Greene and M.D. Herter Norton (New York and London: W.W. Norton, 1947, 1975).

Preface

x   Rilke, *Sonnets to Orpheus*, translated by Daniel Joseph
       Polikoff (Kettering, OH: Angelico Press, 2015).

xi   Ibid., 131.

Introduction

xv   Rilke, *Letters to a Young Poet*, translated by M.D.
       Herter Norton (New York and London: W. W. Norton,
       1954), 29.

xvi   *"Be in advance"*: Rilke, *Sonnets to Orpheus*, II/13.

xxiii *"Do not take pride"*: ibid., II/9.

Part 2 - Old World

6   "The Panther": Rilke, *New Poems*.

14   *"Where is the man"*: *Rilke*, excerpt from "Requiem for
       a Friend" in *The Selected Poetry of Rainer Maria Rilke*,
       translated by Stephen Mitchell (New York: Vintage
       International, 1982), 83, 85.

15   "The Archaic Torso of Apollo": Rilke, *New Poems, The
       Other Part*.

37   "The Cathedral": Rilke, *New Poems*.

38   "The Rose Window": Ibid.

39   "God in the Middle Ages": Ibid.

41   "L'Ange du Meridien": Ibid.

47   MLB, 186-87.

50   "Departure of the Prodigal Son": Rilke, *New Poems*.

53   MLB, 195-96.

64   "Roman Sarcophagi": Rilke, *New Poems*.

65   "The Prisoner": Ibid.

65   "That is how you lost": fragment of the original 10th *Duino Elegy*.

69   "The Angel"; Rilke, *New Poems*.

73   The comments on Les Baux on this and the following page are from Rilke's letter to Witold Hulewicz, Nov. 10, 1925 as provided on p. 310 of *The Selected Poetry of Rainer Maria Rilke,* trans. by Stephen Mitchell.

76   MLB, 213-14.

81   Stephen Mitchell, *The Gospel according to Jesus* (New York: HarperCollins, 1991), 103-104.

82   "Song of the Sea": Rilke, *New Poems, The Other Part*.

87   Rilke, *Letters on Cézanne* (New York, Fromm International: 1985), 34, 4. Letters to Clara Rilke from June 3 and October 9, 1907.

90   "Bowl of Roses": Rilke, *New Poems* (excerpt).

99   Petrarch, Canzoniere XXXV; source of translation unknown.

100 Thomas Cole, letter of Oct. 30, 1941.

102 MLB, 187.

103 "On every Christmas . . . ": Gaspara Stampa translated by Frank Warnke in Warnke, *Three Women Poets of the Renaissance and Baroque* (Bucknell University Press, 1987).

111 GN, 225. Letter to Hans von der Mühll, Oct. 12, 1920.

112 GN, 251. Letter to Princess Marie von Thurn und Taxis-Hohenlohe, July 25, 1921.

113 Ibid., 252-254.

122 GN, 284. Letter to Gertrude Ouckama Knoop, Jan. 1922.

129 Ibid., 315-16. Letter to Countess Margot Sizzo, Jan. 6, 1923.

Part 22 - New World

Coda: A Poet's Parliament

Afterword

Image Credits

Lubbock Avalanche-Journal: Graham photo used on cover

Scott Langley, Death Penalty Photo Documentary Project:
    top left and right on cover; 144, 249, 250, 257

Rothko Chapel, Photos by Hickey-Robertson: 204, 206

iStock: 216

All other photographs and all sketches by
    Daniel Joseph Polikoff

About the Author

Poet, translator, and internationally recognized Rilke scholar Daniel Joseph Polikoff received his Ph.D. in Comparative Literature from Cornell University and his diploma in Waldorf Education from Rudolf Steiner College. In addition to work in numerous literary journals, he has published five books of poetry, translation, and criticism, including *In the Image of Orpheus: Rilke—A Soul History* and a bilingual translation of Rilke's *Sonnets to Orpheus*.

Dr. Polikoff has taught literature in Waldorf high schools as well as courses in literature and depth psychology at Sonoma State University and the California Institute of Integral Studies. He has shared his passion for Rilke in a wide variety of venues in the United States and abroad, including annual meetings of the International Rilke and Jean Gebser Societies, the San Francisco Jung Institute, and the Napa Valley Writer's Conference. His webinars on *Rilke: Poetry and Alchemy* and *Rilke and the Hermetic Tradition* are available through the Asheville Jung Center. He resides with his wife, Monika, and family in the San Francisco Bay area.

More information is available at danielpolikoff.com

CPSIA information can be obtained
at www.ICGtesting.com
Printed in the USA
LVOW05s1914050318
568702LV00016B/519/P